EUROPE

T0382519

Reprinted from
*The Cambridge
Senior Geography*

CAMBRIDGE
UNIVERSITY PRESS

University Printing House, Cambridge CB2 8BS, United Kingdom

Cambridge University Press is part of the University of Cambridge.

It furthers the University's mission by disseminating knowledge in the pursuit of
education, learning and research at the highest international levels of excellence.

www.cambridge.org
Information on this title: www.cambridge.org/9781316612873

© Cambridge University Press 1922

First published 1922
First paperback edition 2016

A catalogue record for this publication is available from the British Library

ISBN 978-1-316-61287-3 Paperback

A GEOGRAPHY OF
EUROPE

(EXCLUDING THE BRITISH ISLES)

By

G. F. BOSWORTH, F.R.G.S.

CAMBRIDGE
AT THE UNIVERSITY PRESS
1922

CONTENTS

LIST OF ILLUSTRATIONS

The illustrations on pp. 146 and 161 are taken from *The Relation of Sculpture to Architecture*, by T. P. Bennett.

EUROPE

Position and Extent.

Europe is the western part of the great land mass known as Eurasia, and is historically and politically the most important of the five continents. In point of size, it is next to Australia the smallest, and is less than one-fourth of the area of Asia, the largest of the continents. From a geological and biological point of view the south of Europe and the north of Africa are very closely related ; indeed, Morocco, Algeria, and Tunis are European rather than African as regards their structure, animals, and plants. On three sides Europe is bounded by the sea : on the north by the Arctic Ocean, on the west by the Atlantic Ocean, and on the south by the Mediterranean Sea, the Sea of Marmora, and the Black Sea. The eastern boundary consists of the Ural Mountains, the Ural River, and the Caspian Sea; but of course these do not mark exact lines of division as regards climate, flora, or fauna. With the exception of a small area within the Arctic circle, the greater part of Europe is within the temperate zone ; the 10th and 66th meridians of west and east longitude, and the 35th and 70th parallels of north latitude roughly mark the limits of the continent, omitting Iceland. The extreme length is 3400 miles measured from Cape St Vincent in Portugal to the mouth of the Kara River ; and the breadth is 2400 miles from North Cape in Norway to Cape Matapan in Greece.

The area is estimated at 3,900,000 square miles. The word *Europe* is variously derived. It is now assumed that the name is from the word *Erebb*, meaning darkness or the land of sunset, which was probably applied by the Phoenicians to the countries which lay to the west of them.

General Features: the Build of Europe.

The physical features of Europe may be broadly considered in three divisions: (1) the highlands of Scandinavia, (2) the highlands of the southern countries, and (3) the great European plain.

(1)   The greater part of Scandinavia is a highland region representing the remains of the ancient plateau of north-western Europe. This highland region reappears in the north-west of Scotland, in Ireland, and in Normandy and Brittany in France.

(2)   The highland region of the south is much loftier and far more extensive, occupying as it does the southern countries and extending northwards to about 51° N. The most important of the southern mountain ranges are the Pyrenees in the west, the Alps forming the centre of this highland region, the Karpathians in the east, the Balkans in the south-east, and the Caucasus range in the far east. This great chain, forming the barrier between France, Germany, and Russia and the Mediterranean countries, has the highest peaks in Europe— Mont Blanc (15,775 feet) in the Alps, and Mount Elbruz in the Caucasus (18,256 feet). The Apennines of Italy and the Pindus of the Balkan peninsula are southern offshoots of this great chain of fold mountains. The peninsula of Spain and Portugal has an ancient plateau—the Meseta; central France has the plateau of Auvergne, consisting of old rocks; and Germany has the Schwarz Wald, the Taunus, the Harz Mountains, and the Erzgebirge, all of which are ancient rocks.

(3)   The great plain of Europe covers at least two-thirds of the continent and extends from England, stretching continuously across Europe, to the Ural

Mountains. It will be noticed that this great plain forms the separation between the two great mountain systems of Europe. In the east, the Netherlands is, in part, below sea level, while the highest land in this plain is found in the Valdai Hills (1100 feet) in Russia.

Volcanoes.

There are three groups of European volcanoes. (1) The more recent and active are found along the Mediterranean in Vesuvius, Etna, the Lipari islands, and Santorin in the Grecian archipelago. (2) The older volcanoes are those of the Auvergne mountains in France, some craters in north-west Germany, and other extinct volcanoes in south Germany. (3) The oldest volcanoes are those in the north-western highlands of Scotland, more particularly in Mull and Skye. This ancient volcanic system is also represented by the volcanic rocks of Antrim in Ireland

Watershed and Rivers.

The main watershed of Europe runs from south-west to north-east, and from it most of the rivers flow northward or southward. The Russian watershed sends the Dvina to the White Sea, the Duna and Niemen to the Baltic, and the Ural, Don, Dnieper, Dniester, and Pruth to the Caspian or Black Seas. The north Russian rivers are of little value from a commercial point of view, as they are blocked with ice for many months, and the same applies in a lesser degree to the Baltic rivers. The Elbe and the Rhine are of great commercial importance ; the former rises 20 miles from the Danube, and the latter near the Rhone, finding its way to the North Sea through a valley. The central plateau of France is the water-shed of the Seine and the Loire, and the Pyrenees give rise to the Garonne and the Adour. The rivers of Spain and Portugal generally work their way across the country through the valleys formed by

Geneva.
(*Pont du Mont Blanc.*)

denudation. The Rhone rises in the Alps near the Rhine and enters the Mediterranean in the gap between the Pyrenees and Hyères. The Po has its course within the curve made by the Alps and the Apennines. The Danube runs through southern Germany and cuts through the mountains into Hungary. A second time, at the Iron Gates, it makes its way through a gorge and after passing through Rumania and Bulgaria, empties itself into the Black Sea.

Lakes.

The "ribbon" lakes of Europe are chiefly confined to mountainous regions and are closely connected with the river system. The Alpine lakes are in the river valleys and have probably been formed by subsidence. This is exemplified both in the Scandinavian and Alpine mountain systems, where long, narrow "ribbon" lakes occupy the lowest parts of some of the valleys, and is particularly well seen in Lakes Constance and Geneva. Here it is thought that the expansion of the river valleys may be due to an earth movement which raised the lower part of the valley and converted the upper part into a closed basin. Some lakes, such as Lake Como or Loch Garry in Scotland, have been caused by the damming up of valleys, and an interesting series of lakes in dammed valleys may be seen in the loch and fjord basins of both Norway and Scotland. Some of the European lakes fill depressions in plains, and of this broad, shallow type many are scattered in north Germany. Lake Balaton in Hungary has an area of 230 square miles and is a good example of lakes filling depressions in plains. The most important of European lakes are those on the plains, and these include the largest lakes in Europe. Ladoga (6960 square miles) in Russia is the largest of all European lakes, and Onega, Peipus, and Ilmen are also in the same country. The lakes of southern Sweden—Wener, Wetter, and Mälar—are in the lowlands and are among the largest in Europe.

On the German shore of the Baltic there are " haffs " or lakes formed along the coast behind beaches and dunes, and among the largest of these are Kurische Haff, and Frische Haff. The present Zuyder Zee was formerly a lake cut off from the sea by a barrier along the line of the Frisian Islands. The largest lake in the British Isles is Lough Neagh, which was formed by a volcanic subsidence.

Coasts.

Many varying estimates of the length of the coast-line of Europe have been made, but the important fact to remember is that it has a greater length of coast-line in proportion to its area than any other continent. Owing to the number and size of the inland seas, every part of the continent is brought into easy communication with the ocean. The northern seas including the Baltic, North, and Irish, are shallow, having a depth that rarely exceeds 600 feet. They are indeed a submerged portion of the great central plain of Europe, and while the outer seas have definite tides, the Baltic is tideless and its waters are not so salt as those of the ocean. The flat, sandy coast of the Baltic forms a striking contrast to the rugged coasts of Norway, Scotland, and Ireland. The southern seas include the Mediterranean, Sea of Marmora, Black Sea, Sea of Azov, and the Caspian Sea. They are landlocked and practically tideless, but deep seas. The Caspian, 85 feet below sea-level, is entirely inland, and its waters are very salt.

Islands.

With the exception of Iceland and Spitzbergen, far out in the ocean, the islands cluster round the mainland. To the north of Russia there is the desolate island of Novaya Zemlya. Norway has deep fjords and innumerable small islands forming the Skagaard. The coast of Sweden has a Skagaard of small islands, but the coast is low and has no deep indentations. The Baltic Sea has several large islands—Gothland, Oland, Zealand, and Funen. The British Isles form the most important group of European islands, which were once joined to the mainland. There is some evidence to show that Scotland was severed from Scandinavia since the appearance of man in north-western Europe. In the Mediterranean Sea there are many islands of interest and importance. Sardinia and Corsica were formerly joined to Italy and are fragments of a land that once occupied the western portion of this great sea. Crete and Cyprus are detached fragments of the Grecian peninsula, and the same is true of the Archipelago of the Ægean Sea.

Climate and Rainfall.

The temperature of Europe increases from north to south, but on reference to a temperature map it will be seen that the isotherms run roughly from north-west to south-east in winter and from south-west to north-east in summer. The south-westerly winds from the Atlantic produce a warm temperature running northward along the coast of Scandinavia ; and the influence of these south-westerly winds and the equalizing effect of the Atlantic ocean render the variations between summer and winter temperatures less marked in western than in eastern Europe. Thus the plains of southern Russia have shorter and hotter summers, and colder and longer winters, than places in the same latitude in western Europe. The lands around the Mediterranean have a warmer, sunnier climate than that in the north of the Alps. Dry winds blow across the Mediterranean in the summer towards the Sahara, but at certain seasons the Mediterranean coast is subject to the Sirocco, a hot, sand-laden wind from the same region. The general temperature of Europe and the local temperature in particular districts is influenced by the elevation of the land. To illustrate this fact it may be mentioned that, while the summit

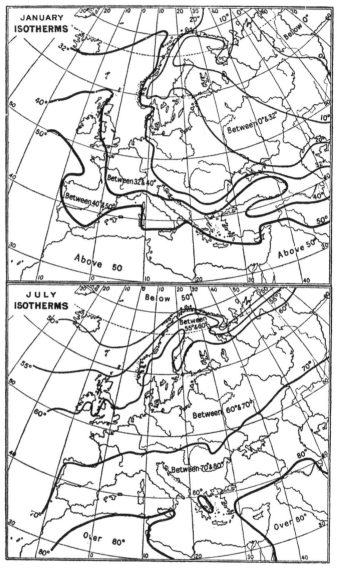

Isotherms of Europe.

of Mont Blanc may have 20° of frost, the valley at its base may, at the same time, have a temperature of 70° F.

As a general rule, the rainfall of western Europe is greater than that of the eastern plains. Of course mountains always produce a considerably higher rainfall locally, and the highest rainfall in Europe generally occurs to the south and west of the mountains and on their western and southern slopes. The distribution of the rainfall is fairly equal throughout the year, but the greatest contrast is that between the eastern plains and the Mediterranean region. In the former district the summer rains are most abundant while the winter rains are scanty. Lisbon has 29 ins. of rain to Madrid's 16 ins. Bordeaux has 33 ins. of rainfall, Berlin 23 ins., and Moscow 21 ins. The rainfall of parts of Ireland, Scotland, and Wales is the heaviest in Europe and in some places reaches 200 ins., while the north and south-east of Russia are among the driest districts of the continent.

Plants.

The climate of a country is the most potent factor in determining the use that can be made of its soil. Hence in considering the plants, it will be well to remember that the rainfall is generally heaviest in the west and gradually decreases eastward to the Russian plain. The temperature of north-western and western Europe, being raised by the proximity of the ocean and the prevailing south-westerly wind, has a marked effect on the plant life. Plants which require a mild winter will not grow in the north, but advance along the western coast under the influence of the maritime climate. Thus the myrtle, not an indigenous plant, grows even in the south of England. Many of the European plants have been introduced from Africa or from the east; this has been the case certainly with the vine, olive, orange, lemon, fig, peach, almond, and apricot, and probably with the

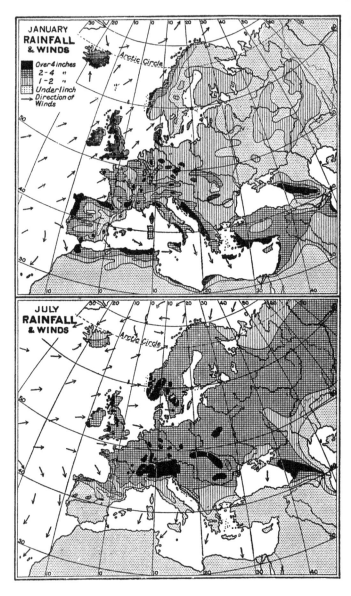

Rainfall and winds of Europe.

myrtle. All these are thoroughly characteristic of the Mediterranean region, and to them may be added the cactus and the agave. In south-eastern Europe and in Hungary there are steppes—great treeless plains with coarse grasses and scanty shrubs.

The trees of Europe are of the greatest commercial importance, and the forests of Russia, Scandinavia, and Germany are most extensive. Spruce firs, pines, and larches flourish in the north, and about 60° N. lat. the conifers are supplanted by deciduous trees having broader leaves. Among the deciduous trees of central Europe are the alder, beech, birch, chestnut, elm, lime, oak, sycamore, and plane, all of which are better adapted for the warmer conditions of life. A great deciduous forest formerly stretched to the Mediterranean, but much of it has been cleared, and now the trees do not form great forests but are scattered in clumps over the district. The most common trees in this southern region are the laurel, holly, myrtle, mulberry, and olive—trees with glossy leaves and retentive of moisture.

In the north-east of Europe is the tundra region, where an Arctic flora of mosses and lichens prevails.

Animals.

The wild animals are fast decreasing as the forests are being cleared and the land is brought under cultivation. Among the wild animals there yet remain the reindeer, elk, and Polar bear in the north ; the stag, the fallow deer, and the roebuck in the more southern regions; and the ibex is found on the central mountains. The animals peculiar to Europe are the chamois, musk rat, and fallow deer, and of the carnivorous animals the most noteworthy are the bear, wolf, fox, and lynx. The domestic animals used for food, clothing, or means of transport are found largely on the grass lands; this is especially true of cattle, sheep, and horses. The horse, mule, ox, camel, and reindeer are used as beasts of burden in different parts of the continent.

The European seas and rivers afford excellent fisheries; the most valuable are those of the North Sea from which cod, herring, and mackerel are obtained in immense quantities. The tunny and anchovy fisheries of the Mediterranean are of lesser importance. Salmon are caught in rivers of the north-west, particularly in Norway and Scotland, and sturgeon in the rivers of the south-east and the Caspian Sea.

The Economic Resources of Europe.

The minerals of greatest economic importance are those used as fuel and those worked for metals. Coal is the most important of the minerals used as fuel, and the European coalfields are widely scattered in the north European plain and the neighbouring islands. The coalfields along the Mediterranean region have, so far, proved unimportant. Black coal is found in the rocks of the carboniferous system, especially in the British Isles, France, Belgium, and western Germany. Brown coal is softer than black coal and of less value as a fuel. It is mined in south Germany and Austria. Petroleum wells are common in south-east Russia along the shores of the Caspian Sea, especially at Baku, the chief oil-field. Iron is by far the most useful and most important metal of Europe, and is often found in the neighbourhood of coal-mines, which, of course, much increases its value. The iron industry was founded in the British Isles where large quantities of the ore exist, and Spain, Scandinavia, south Germany, and parts of France also yield large supplies. One of the oldest metals used by man is copper and this is now obtained from south Spain, Italy, Germany, Wales, and Cornwall. Tin in ancient times was obtained from the Cornish mines, and Dolcoath mine, one of the greatest tin mines in Europe, is still being worked. Lead comes from Spain, Derbyshire, Wales, south Scotland, and the Harz and Erzgebirge mountains in Germany. Mercury is obtained from Spanish ores, and sulphur from volcanic districts, particularly Sicily and Stromboli. Rock salt is mined from rocks of the European plain, especially in Britain, central Germany, and Austria, and much salt is obtained by evaporation along the sea coast of France and other countries. Europe is not rich in the precious metals; the chief gold mines are in the Ural Mountains and in Hungary; silver is more widely distributed and is generally found in lead ores; and platinum is chiefly found in the Urals.

It has already been noted that the Mediterranean lands have a warmer and more genial climate than further north, and as a result they produce fruits, oil-bearing plants, and the vine, which also grows freely in France and southern Germany. The vine is grown on the southern slopes of the hills and is found as far as 50° N. lat. Wheat grows best in limestone districts, especially in countries between latitudes 45° and 54°. The southern part of England, northern France, Germany, Hungary, and south Russia are the best wheat-producing areas. Barley and rye grow farther north than wheat, while maize, which requires a higher temperature, is cultivated farther south. Among the vegetables, potatoes and beet are the two most important root-crops; the former thrive in Ireland, south Scandinavia, and north Germany, the latter in north France, Germany, and south Russia.

The extensive grass lands of Europe consist mainly of rich meadow lands in England, Denmark, and Holland which support cattle and dairy farms, and the wide, open, dry plains, especially the Russian steppes, devoted to sheep-rearing and other industries.

People, Distribution of Population. Race. Religion.

The population of Europe may be estimated at 400,000,000 and is second among the continents to that of Asia, although, in proportion to its area, it is the most densely peopled. The population is most sparse in

Scandinavia, Russia, and the north of Scotland.   The
large aggregations of people occur in the neighbourhood
of mining and manufacturing towns, or at seaports
and in their vicinity.   The great majority of the
people belong to the Caucasic or white division of
the human family.   It was conjectured by Keane that
the original home of the white race was in North
Africa between the Sudan and the Mediterranean,

Lapp Encampment.

and the same authority estimates the white people
of Europe to number 355,000,000.   At least 90 per
cent. of this total speak languages belonging to the
Greco-Italic, the Teutonic, and the Slavonic stocks
of the Aryan group.   It is probable that the number
of the Teutons and Slavs is about equal, although

the latter have been increasing very rapidly of late, while the people speaking the languages belonging to the Greco-Italic stock are the least numerous of the three. Celtic languages are spoken in Wales, the Scottish highlands, Ireland, and Brittany; and Lettic and Lithuanian in West Russia. The Magyars of Hungary, the Turks and Tatars of the Russian steppes, and the Finns and Lapps of the extreme north are non-Aryan and belong to the Mongolian race.

With the exception of the Turks, who are Mohammedans, the bulk of the European people are Christians. Western Europe still shows traces of the influence of the Roman Empire, while Eastern Europe belongs to the Greek Church. Speaking broadly it may be said that southern Europe belongs to the Roman Catholic Church, while the Teutonic people broke away from this Church in the sixteenth century and profess some form of Protestantism. The separation of the Eastern and Western Churches which began in 330 A.D., when Constantinople became the capital of the East, was completed in the ninth century. The Turks captured Constantinople in 1453, and Luther inaugurated the Reformation at Wittenberg in 1517. Jews are scattered all over Europe, but are most numerous in Poland, Russia, Austria, and Germany.

France.

Position and Extent.

In shape France is roughly pentagonal, and is well situated between the Atlantic on the west to the Mediterranean on the south. The English Channel and the Straits of Dover form the separation from England, the two opposite coasts approaching within 21 miles of each other between Dover and Calais. The Pyrenees are a very definite physical boundary separating France and Spain on the south; while Belgium, Luxemburg, Germany, Switzerland, and Italy are on the

north-east and east.   The area, including Corsica,
is about 213,000 square miles ; the greatest length is
606 miles from north to south, and the greatest breadth
556 miles.   France lost Alsace and part.of Lorraine
to Germany in 1871, but has since regained them and
acquired colonies which now extend to upwards of
5,000,000 square miles, chiefly in Asia and Africa.   Of
these, Algeria is fast becoming a part of France, and is
counted as such for purposes of administration.

Surface and General Features.

The greater part of France consists of plains and
undulating land, while the lofty Pyrenees and the Alps
form the land frontier on the south and south-east.
The French Jura and the Vosges on the eastern frontier
are higher than any British mountains ; and Mont
Blanc (15,780 feet) in the Alps belongs to France.   The
chief highlands within the French frontier belong to
the central plateau, which has an average elevation
of 2500 to 3000 feet and ends in the Cevennes, over-
looking the Rhone valley.   The whole of north-western
France, except a few hilly tracts in La Vendée, Brittany,
and Normandy, is covered with wide plains.   Specially
noteworthy is an extensive sandy region known as the
Landes, extending between the Bay of Biscay, the Adour,
and the Loire.   This district is now intersected with
canals and planted with trees, and is no longer a malarial
region.   The Auvergne is a central hilly district with
several summits that were formerly volcanoes, of which
Mont Dore (6188 feet) is the highest.   It will be evident
from a glance at the map that the coast line of France is
relatively short, and there are really few good harbours.
Its northern coast bears some affinity to the southern
coast of England, but the only striking scenery is in
Brittany, the counterpart, to some extent, of Cornwall
and Devon.   On the seaward side the extensive region
of the Landes is fringed by salt lagoons.   The Riviera
coast, to the east of Toulon, especially at Cannes and
Nice, is strikingly beautiful and is the resort in winter of

the wealthy. Except Corsica, France has no islands
of importance, and those off the coast of Brittany and
the Mediterranean are only detached portions of the
mainland. The Channel Islands, between Brittany and
the Cotentin peninsula, belong to Britain—the sole
remnant of our once extensive French possessions.

Watersheds and Rivers.

The central plateau forms the great watershed and
from it flow, with one exception, all the chief rivers,
generally in a westerly direction. The Rhone is the
exception and, coming into France from Switzerland,
it is the only river flowing south. The rapidity of its
current lessens its commercial value. Its valley is
between the Alps and the Cevennes and it enters the
Gulf of Lions by a delta. France is a remarkably well-
watered country, and its rivers are generally navigable.
On the western side, the little Adour fringes the Landes,
and the Dordogne and Garonne unite to form the
Gironde, a fine marine estuary. The Loire, the longest
river, drains one-fifth of France and becomes a great
river after receiving the Allier. The Seine, the chief
French river, flows through a wide basin, which this
river and its tributaries have made the dominant part
of the country from earliest historical times. The importance of the river navigation of France is shown by
the fact that all the great westerly-flowing rivers are
connected, directly or indirectly, with the Rhine or
Rhone.

Climate and Rainfall.

France has the advantage of a westerly maritime
situation, together with a more southerly latitude than
the British Isles, and it is therefore natural that it
should have more sunshine. On the central highlands,
however, the climate is more extreme and drier than
on the west. On the whole, France has a very fine
climate, and while not so continental as that of its
neighbour on the east, it is not so maritime as that of

The Loire at Orleans.

England. The climate of Brittany is very similar to that of south-west England, and Pau, on the slopes of the Pyrenees, is deservedly famous as a health resort. The difference in altitude causes many kinds of climate to be encountered, from the mouth of the Loire, where frosts are unknown, to the summit of Mont Blanc with its perpetual snow. The range of temperature at Paris is somewhat wide at certain periods, and has been known to vary from 13° F. in winter to 95° F. in the summer. The rainfall is considerable on the western plains and generally decreases towards the east. The mean annual rainfall of France is about 29 inches, and while the Mediterranean coast district has a maximum of less than 20 inches, the Vosges district has 60 inches and the western portion of the Pyrenees has a maximum of 71 inches. The climate of Languedoc and Provence has to some extent an African character, for a temperate winter is succeeded by a torrid summer, moderated at times by the mistral.

Plants and Animals.

As we might expect from the varying climate owing to the difference of altitude and exposure, the flora of France is rich. The chief forest trees are the oak, beech, elm, and maple, while the pine and fir are common to the mountains and sandy regions. Provence, in the south-east, is the garden of France and there eucalyptus, olive, and mulberry thrive. Throughout the country many types of vegetation are found, from the vines of the Medoc to the woods and pastures of the Alps. The wild animals are decreasing owing to the comparative lack of forest land, and bears, wolves, and chamois are found only in the lonely mountainous or wooded regions.

Agricultural Products.

About seven-tenths of the surface is cultivated land divided up into very small farms, and about half the surface is arable land. Nearly half the working population is engaged in agriculture and the peasant farmers work with great industry. Of the cereals, wheat is the chief grain crop, grown in all parts, but especially north of the Seine. Oats are grown in the north and north-east; rye is the chief grain of the central plateau; maize is grown in the Rhone valley and in the south-west; and buckwheat in the north-east. The vine, however, is the typical cultivated plant, and there are vineyards in all parts, except a strip on the north-west coast and on the central plateau. The chief wine-producing departments are Hérault, Garde and Aude on the Mediterranean, Gironde on the Bay of Biscay, and the Burgundy district. Reims is the centre of the Champagne district. Of late years, owing to the devastation wrought by the phylloxera, there has been a decrease in the production of wine, and a large amount is imported from Spain, Italy, and Algeria. The olive and mulberry trees are cultivated in the south, and the beet-crop of the north is of great value. Colza, hemp, flax, and tobacco are crops of some importance. Cattle are fed on the western plains, and sheep on the poor pastures of the central plateau. Oxen are used in agricultural work, and donkeys and mules are often the beasts of burden in the south.

Fisheries.

Fishing occupies about 130,000 men round the coasts, especially off Normandy and Brittany. Dunkirk and Nantes are the two chief ports, and large vessels visit Newfoundland and Iceland for cod. Oyster culture is of some importance on the sandy Atlantic coast, especially at Arcachon and on the Mediterranean coast. Tunny fishing is carried on around Corsica.

Minerals.

The mineral resources of France are much inferior to those of Britain, and this is most evident in the case of coal, for at least half the quantity used is imported.

The best coal-mines are in the Valenciennes field in the north, and the central coal-fields, including the mines about St Etienne and Le Creusot, come next in importance. Iron is abundant and is generally found near the coal. Lead from the Auvergne Mountains is the only other metal of importance. Good building stone is quarried in Brittany, Normandy, and elsewhere; and there are salt-mines on the west and south, but one-half the supply comes from the salt marshes on the shores of the Bay of Biscay and the Mediterranean. In some parts of France, especially in the regions of extinct volcanoes, there are thermo-mineral springs, some of which are of considerable value and are yearly visited by large numbers of patients.

Industries and Manufactures.

Owing to the deficiency of coal, France is not so favoured as Britain as an industrial nation. The most productive French coal-field has its centre near Valenciennes. The blast-furnaces and steel-works of St Etienne and Le Creusot have immense iron-foundries and engineering establishments. In point of value the most important manufactures are wool and silk, the former carried on chiefly in the north, and the latter in the south. It will be found that the textile industries flourish in the neighbourhood of the coal-fields or near the supply of raw materials. Thus the woollen industry is localised chiefly in the department Nord, and one-third of the whole is done at Roubaix, Tourcoing, and Fourmies. The silk trade is largely carried on near Lyons, which is the greatest silk market in the world. St Etienne has extensive ribbon factories; Rouen is the French Manchester, with the chief cotton mills of France; Lille is the centre of the linen trade; Amiens has velvet factories and makes much cotton. Lace-making is a characteristic French home industry, the chief centres being Alençon, Bayeux, and Calais. Porcelain is made at Limoges and Sèvres, and carpets at Gobelins. There are also sugar works, chemical industries, paper mills, and industries connected with dress, furniture, and all articles of luxury. In all these industries the French display inventive genius and artistic taste, and Paris is the emporium for these articles.

Communications.

The French highways are kept in an excellent state, and besides the 24,000 miles of *routes nationales*, there are twice as many miles of *routes départmentales* and *chemins vicinaux*. The canal and river system of France is very complete, and is of much more importance than that of England. At least one-third of the inland goods traffic is by means of canals and rivers. The *Canal du Midi*, 150 miles long, runs from Bordeaux to Toulouse and thence to Cette, thus saving a sea-passage of 2000 miles. The Rhone is joined through the Saône by a canal to the Rhine, by another to the Loire, and by a third to the Seine. The canal traffic is heaviest in the north, where there is a network of water-ways. The railway system radiates from Paris, which is seven hours from London by the Calais-Dover passage.

The chief lines are :

1. The *Northern* to Boulogne, Calais, Lille, and other northern towns, with connections to Brussels, Berlin, and Petrograd.

2. The *Western* to Rouen, Havre, Dieppe, Cherbourg, and Brest.

3. The *Paris-Orleans* serves the area between the Loire and the Garonne ; the chief centres are Orleans, Tours, and Poitiers.

4. The *Southern Lines*, of which one runs into Spain by Bayonne, and another by Toulouse to Cette.

5. The *Paris, Lyons*, and *Mediterranean* has the greatest traffic, with stations at Dijon, Mâcon (the centre for the Mont Cenis tunnel route to Italy), Lyons, and Marseilles.

6. The *Eastern* has one line through Chalons and Nancy leading to Germany, and another goes through Belfort into Alsace and Switzerland, connecting with

Austria by the Arlberg tunnel and with Italy by the St Gothard tunnel.

Commerce and Trade.

The chief imports of raw textile materials are wool, silk, and cotton, and these, with wine, grain and flour, coal and coke, together make up one-third of the total value. The chief exports comprise woollen, cotton, and silk goods, and after these, leather goods, spirits, wine, and chemicals are of importance. Great Britain stands first among the customers of France. It receives one-quarter of the exports from France, and sends one-seventh of the imports. Belgium, Germany, and the United States rank next in order. The French mercantile marine carries only one-quarter of the French commerce, and there is a high tariff on imported goods.

People and History.

In the early days, France was peopled by the Gauls, the dominant race, the Ligurians on the Mediterranean, and the Iberians or Basques in the south-west. These were conquered by the Romans, and after the campaign of Caesar the Gauls adopted the Latin speech and Roman manners and mode of life. In the fourth century, Gaul came under the power of Teutonic invaders, especially the Burgundians, the Visigoths, and the Franks. Clovis the Frank laid the foundations of the future kingdom of France, and later Charlemagne ruled over this country, but his power faded under his successors. Paris became the capital in the tenth century, and the Northmen settled in Normandy. In the succeeding centuries the kings of England were also Dukes of Normandy and were more powerful than the native rulers. English power in France ended in 1451, when only Calais was left to England of all her possessions, and that was finally lost in the reign of Mary. The eighteenth century was a period of rivalry between France and Britain both in the Old World and America, and Napoleon's power was overthrown at Waterloo in

1815. The line of the Bourbons was restored in 1814,
and the *coup d'état* of 1852 inaugurated the second
empire of Napoleon III, which lasted till the disastrous
Franco-German war of 1870–71.   Then a Republic was
constituted which has since continued to govern the
country.   The later years of the nineteenth century
saw the extension of the French colonial empire, and
succeeding years were memorable by reason of the
entente cordiale with Britain.   The Great War of 1914
was closed by an Armistice on November 11, 1918. The
Peace of Versailles (June 28, 1919) gave France the
provinces of Alsace and Lorraine, and the Rhine once
again became the boundary of the French Republic.

There are about 39 million people in France and the
density to the square mile is nearly 190.   The rural
population to the urban is as 22 : 17.   There are
15 towns with populations of over 100,000; Paris has
2¾ millions, and Marseilles, the second town, has half a
million.

The Geographical Advantages of France.

The geographical advantages of France have enabled
it to play a leading part in the history of modern
Europe, and next to England she is the most favourably
situated of all the European countries.   The geographical conditions that give France so many advantages in
her rivalry with other European nations may be briefly
summarised.   (1) The northern coast is washed by the
narrow sea which is the greatest highway of the world's
commerce.   (2) The western coast is open to the
Atlantic and the southern coast to the Mediterranean.
(3) The harbours on all the coasts are adequate and the
rivers are generally navigable.   (4) The soil is more
fertile than that of most European countries.   (5) The
mountain frontiers in the south and south-east afford
protection on those sides, though they do not entirely
impede peaceful intercourse.   (6) The compact shape of
France tends to the unity of the country.   (7) Brittany
is the one section that has been separately influenced

by its geography, and as a result it has been remote
from the general life of France. There a Celtic language
still survives, and the people retain the ideas and tra-
ditions of the past.

Administration and Divisions.

France is a republic under a President, who is
elected every seven years, and two houses of parliament,
the Senate and the Chamber of Deputies, which unitedly
form the National Assembly or Congress. For purposes
of administration France is divided into 90 departments
under prefects, and these are further subdivided into
arrondissements under sub-prefects, and communes
under mayors. Many of the departments are named
after their rivers or mountains, such as Seine-et-Marne,
Indre-et-Loire, Basses-Alpes, and Hautes-Pyrenées; and
some after the aspect of the country, as the Landes.
For purposes of voting there is manhood suffrage. The
standing army is the result of conscription, and there
is a large navy.

Towns.

Paris, the capital of France, is divided by the Seine
into two parts, and is situated in the centre of a rich
region. It is the most populous city of France, and
ranks after London and New York as one of the world's
greatest cities. It is a great industrial and commercial
centre, its fine position giving it easy communication
with all parts of France, and with England, Belgium,
and Germany. Paris is surrounded by fortifications,
through which pass the railways which radiate over
the country. *Marseilles*, the second city, on the
Mediterranean, is the chief harbour, having a large
trade with Mediterranean ports and via the Suez
Canal with India, China, and Australia. *Havre*, on
the Seine, is the second seaport, having a large trade
in coffee and cotton with the northern French ports,
England, and America. *Bordeaux*, on the Garonne, is
the chief wine port of France. *Dunkirk, Calais,*

Boulogne, and *Dieppe* are seaports that trade with
English and North Sea ports. *Lille*, a fortress near
Belgium, is an industrial town famous for its machinery,
sugar, and chemicals. *Toulouse*, on the Garonne, is
well situated between the Atlantic and the Mediterranean. It is the centre of a rich agricultural district
and its people are distinguished for their taste in letters
and arts. *St Etienne* has grown into importance in

Reims: the Cathedral in July, 1918.

recent years and manufactures machinery, hardware,
and silk ribbons. *Lyons*, at the confluence of the Rhone
and the Saône, is the chief seat of the silk trade. *Nantes*
is a seaport on the Loire, but owing to its sandbanks,
St Nazaire, nearer the ocean, has taken some of its
trade. The two ports are now connected by a ship canal.
Nice, near the Italian frontier, has a delightful climate
and is a famous winter resort. *Rouen*, on the Seine,
has considerable trade and its manufacture of cotton

goods is of great importance. *Cherbourg*, at the extremity
of the Cotentin peninsula, and *Brest*, at the extreme
western end of Brittany, are naval and military towns of
the first importance on the Atlantic. *Toulon* is of similar
importance on the Mediterranean. *Reims*, formerly
the place of coronation of French kings, is renowned
for its cathedral, one of the finest extant specimens of
Gothic architecture; but owing to the constant bom-
bardment of this city by the Germans during the Great
War this cathedral suffered irreparable damage. Besides
having large woollen manufactures, Reims is the principal entrepôt for the wines of Champagne. *Strassburg*,
in Alsace, on the Ill, but quite close to the Rhine, has
breweries and tobacco factories.

Belgium.

Position and Extent.

Belgium, one of the smallest European states, is the
southern portion of the former kingdom of the Netherlands, and lies between France and Holland, the North
Sea and Rhenish Prussia. Its area of 11,744 square
miles is about one-third of that of Ireland, and its
greatest length from north-west to south-east is 175
miles. As a result of the Great War, Germany was made
to cede to Belgium the districts of Eupen, Moresnet,
and Malmédy.

Surface and General Features.

The sea-coast is only about 40 miles in length and
the depth of the sea is not more than 30 feet within a
distance of five miles from the shore. The surface of
Belgium in the south-east is a tableland; this is watered
by the Meuse, and the slope of the land is towards the
plains in the north and west, where it is flat throughout
the provinces of Flanders, Antwerp, and Limburg. The
high and picturesque plateau of the Ardennes rises to
a height of 2000 feet, but on the southern border the

land is not more than 1000 feet above sea-level. The
great navigable rivers, the Scheldt and Meuse, both rise
in France, but their mouths are in Holland. Both rivers
have numerous tributaries, and there are nearly 600
miles of canals. A district known as the Campine,
composed of marshes and heaths, extends along the
Dutch frontier; and in Flanders the encroachments of
the sea are checked by dykes.

Climate and Productions.

Belgium lies between 49½° and 51½° N., and Brussels
has the same mean temperature, 50° F., as London,
which is in latitude 51½° N. Generally, the climate is cool
and equable ; the district of the Ardennes has greater
extremes, and there the mean temperature is 45°. The
prevailing winds from the west and south-west explain
the fact that rain falls on 195 days in the year. The
rainfall in the Ardennes region is higher than elsewhere
in Belgium. About three-fourths of Belgium is under
cultivation, the principal crops being wheat, rye, and
oats ; and the less important, beet (especially sugar-
beet), buckwheat, and flax. Flax is grown chiefly
in the valley of the Lys, the water of which, being free
from lime salts, is well suited for cleansing the fibre.
About one-sixth of Belgium is forest land, and there
is a good area under pasture, especially in the rich
meadows of the low provinces. The land is cultivated
by the farmers, most of whom are small holders who
have gained a high position for the laborious care they
have taken in making the most of the soil.

Belgium is rich in minerals, especially coal and zinc.
The most productive coal-fields are in the area round
Mons, near the French frontier, and round Charleroi
in eastern Hainault. The Belgian coal-fields are more
difficult to work than the British, for they lie at a
greater depth and are not so continuous. Iron ore
is obtained from Namur, Liège, and Luxemburg; zinc
from Moresnet ; lead from Verviers ; slate from Luxemburg ; and stone from Brabant, Hainault, and Namur.

The breeding of horses in Belgium is of great importance; the great Flemish and Brabant breeds and the smaller Ardennes horse are famous.

People, Industries, and Communications.

Belgium is one of the most densely peopled countries in Europe. Its population of 7,600,000 gives an average of 660 to the square mile. The people are crowded together in the industrial centres, and the Ardennes district has the smallest population. The Belgians are partly of Romanic and partly of Teutonic origin, and speak two languages, Flemish and French, the latter being the official language. This explains the fact that most Belgian towns have a Flemish and a French name. Belgium was for five centuries under the Romans, and then passed under the sway of the Franks, the Burgundians, the Austrians, and the French. In 1815 Belgium and Holland were united, but in 1830 the former became an independent country. Almost all the people are Roman Catholics. The manufactures are of considerable importance, largely owing to the mineral wealth. The linen manufacture at Ghent and Tournai, in the valley of the Lys, has been already mentioned; and the woollen manufacture is carried on chiefly in the northwest, especially at Liège. Machinery is made in the neighbourhood of Liège and Charleroi, fire-arms at Liège, and cutlery and glass on or near the coal-fields. Lace is made at Brussels, Malines, and Bruges. Belgium is a busy and prosperous commercial country, and for its size has the longest and most complete railway system in Europe. The lines of steam-vessels connect Antwerp with most of the commercial countries of the world, and there are daily services between Ostend and Dover, and between Antwerp and Harwich. Its railways bring it into communication with France, Switzerland, and Italy, and with Berlin, Vienna, Petrograd, and Constantinople. Brussels is the centre of the railways, which are mostly state-owned.

Belgium exports iron, machinery, grain, coal, flax,

linen, wool, hides, zinc, glass, and chemicals; and imports wheat, wool, timber, and coffee. The neighbouring countries have the largest share of the foreign trade, but the United States is increasing its trade with Belgium.

Brussels: the Museum of Painting and Sculpture.

Administration and Towns.

The king is the head of the constitutional monarchy, and the legislative body consists of the Senate and the Chamber of Representatives. The country has nine provinces, which are divided into 41 arrondissements, and then again into communes.

The capital of Belgium is *Brussels*, which has of late years been transformed into a beautiful city, with broad thoroughfares and fine modern buildings. Its ancient buildings, notably the Hôtel de Ville and the houses of the old guilds, are of great architectural importance. Besides being the residence of the king and the seat of government, Brussels is an intellectual and industrial centre. *Antwerp*, on the Scheldt, 60 miles from the sea, is one of the great commercial seaports of Europe. *Liège* owes its industrial prosperity to the neighbouring coal mines. It is strongly fortified and has manufactures of fire-arms, besides the industries connected with the Royal Arsenal and other engineering works. Its famous siege in August, 1914, was the dramatic opening of the Great War. *Ghent*, at the confluence of the Lys and Scheldt, is a town of considerable historical importance, although it is now mainly an industrial centre. *Ostend*, a seaport in West Flanders, is connected by a canal with the old seaport of *Bruges*, a decayed but glorious city of the Middle Ages.

Holland.

Position and Extent.

Holland is the popular name of the country known officially as the Netherlands. This little maritime kingdom of about 12,600 square miles is bounded by the North Sea, Prussia, and Belgium. The area varies from time to time owing to encroachments by the sea and to reclamations from the sea. In 1894 the area of land destroyed by the sea was greater than the provinces of North Brabant and Limburg. Till 1890 Luxemburg was connected with Holland, but it is now an independent Grand Duchy.

Surface and General Features.

Holland is not only flat but much of it lies below the level of the sea. It is mainly a delta formed by the Rhine, Meuse, and Scheldt, which flow through it into

A Dutch Canal.

the North Sea. There is no highland region, and two-fifths of the surface would be flooded by the sea if it were not protected by dunes and dykes. Some of the lower tracts, from five to 15 feet below sea-level, are protected by broad and flat embankments which are used as carriage roads and footpaths. The most characteristic feature of Holland is the network of canals, which are navigable for small craft, help to irrigate the land, and in winter are splendid iceways. Many canals connect the parallel rivers and it is possible to travel on water throughout the whole of Holland. It is worth noting that one of the public departments is the Waterstaat, whose functions are the cutting and maintaining of dykes and canals and the formation of " polders," or nearly water-tight enclosures. The most important canals are the North Sea Canal from Amsterdam to the sea, the North Holland Canal from Amsterdam to Den Helder, and the " New Waterway," which enables ocean steamers to reach Rotterdam at all times.

Holland has no rivers entirely her own, and the larger rivers flow from south-east to north-west, which is the direction of the slope of the country. The Rhine and the Waal have been international waterways since 1869.

The chief features of the western coast are sand-banks, mud flats, embankments, and sand dunes. The inlets, the Zuider Zee and the Dollart Zee, were formed by inroads of the sea in the thirteenth and fourteenth centuries, and there is now a scheme for the reclamation of the former at an estimated cost of £16,000,000.

Climate and Productions.

The climate of Holland is somewhat like that of eastern England, but as a rule the Dutch summer is hotter and the winter colder. It will be noted that Amsterdam has the same latitude as Yarmouth. The mean annual temperature is 50° F. and the yearly rainfall is 28 inches. The reclaimed lands are the least healthy parts and there ague is common.

Cattle-rearing and dairy-farming are the chief occupations. The soil of the polder regions is naturally moist and produces rich pasture grasses, so that horses and cattle are numerous, and the cows give abundance of milk. Rye, buckwheat, and potatoes grow on the sandy soils, and elsewhere hops, rape-seed, sugar-beet, tobacco, and wheat are cultivated. There is a small area devoted to orchards, and the culture of Dutch bulbs at and round Haarlem is a characteristic of the country.

People, Industries, and Trade.

The Dutch belong to the Low German branch of the Teutonic race and trace their origin to the Frisians, the Saxons, and the Franks. The country was conquered by the Romans, was under the rule of the dukes of Burgundy, separated from the German Empire, and enjoyed self government under Charles V. After a long war of independence against Spain, Holland was recognised as a free republic in 1648. The seventeenth century was high water mark for Holland as a nation, for then it was that Dutch commerce, science, classical scholarship, literature, and art stood pre-eminent, and it was in the middle of that century when Holland and England were rivals at sea. French armies overran Holland at the time of the French Revolution, and in 1806 Louis Napoleon was made king of Holland. On the fall of Napoleon, Holland and Belgium were united, but Belgium seceded from the union in 1830.

Holland formerly was noted for its manufacturing industry, but the absence of minerals militates against the carrying on of manufactures by machinery, although cotton, linen, and woollen spinning and weaving are pursued to some extent.

At least one-third of the workers are occupied on the land, and, besides the textile workers, others are employed in ship-building, the making of paper and leather, and the preparation of sugar, spirits, and food materials, especially butter and cheese. Fishing is of some importance and is carried on chiefly in the North Sea, although many fishermen work in the Zuider Zee and in the rivers of South Holland and Zealand.

Holland has stood in the front rank of commercial nations since the end of the sixteenth century, and its trade is chiefly with Germany, the United Kingdom, Belgium, the Dutch East Indies, and Russia. The foreign and inland trade and commerce are facilitated by the network of roads and dykes, tramways, and railways; and the waterways, natural and artificial, are of greater relative importance than in any other European country.

Administration and Towns.

Holland is a limited constitutional monarchy; the crown is the executive power and legislation is vested in the States-General of two chambers. The country is divided into 11 provinces and 1110 communes. There is no state religion, and the universities are at Leyden, Utrecht, Groningen, and Amsterdam.

Amsterdam is the commercial capital, famous for its exchange, its shipping, and diamond-cutting. *Rotterdam* is the chief seaport, and since 1872 has been connected with the sea by a ship canal. The *Hook of Holland* has a daily steam service with Harwich. *Flushing* is on the mail route from England to Holland. *The Hague* is the capital of the kingdom. *Schiedam* manufactures gin, and *Delft* makes fine pottery.

Germany.

Position and Size.

Germany is the English name of the country which its natives call Deutschland and which the French call Allemagne. The name is given to the country of which Prussia is the head, although it is sometimes used in a broader sense when it includes the area of the European continent within which the Germanic race and language are predominant. In its present political sense, Germany occupies the central portion of Europe; the sea boundaries are the North Sea from Holland to Denmark, and the Baltic from Denmark to Russia; elsewhere it is bounded by Denmark on the north, Poland and Czecho-Slovakia on the east, Austria and Switzerland on the south, and by France, Belgium, and Holland on the west. Its area is 250,000 square miles.

Surface and General Features.

The north and the greater part of east Germany consists of a great plain, while the remainder of the country is mainly hilly country and tablelands.   It will be noticed that the mountains of Germany are chiefly on the frontier and are generally short ranges.   The most important mountains are the Harz in the north ; the Taunus, Thüringerwald, Erzgebirge, and Riesengebirge in the middle; and the Schwarzwald (Black Forest) and Bavarian Alps in the south.   The highest peak of Germany, Zugspitze (9710 feet), is in the latter range, and Schneekoppe in the Riesengebirge reaches 5266 feet.

Along the North Sea there is a low coastal plain separated from the beach by sand-dunes. Here the sea is encroaching and has already separated the Frisian Islands from the mainland.   The coasts both of the North Sea and the Baltic are extremely shallow, and owing to the sandbanks are well marked by buoys and lights. A ship canal across Jutland from the Elbe to Kiel was opened in 1895, and now the largest steamers may pass between the North Sea and the Baltic.   The length of this "Kaiser Wilhelm Canal" is 61 miles, and it effects a saving in distance of 237 miles and in time of 22 hours for steamers. By the Treaty of Versailles it is provided that this canal shall be maintained free and open to vessels of commerce or war of all nations at peace with Germany.

Watersheds, Rivers, and Lakes.

There are three drainage basins. The greater part of Bavaria is drained by the Danube, which has its source in the Black Forest and pours its waters into the Black Sea. As the larger portion of Germany has a northern slope, it will be found that the remaining rivers flow to the North Sea and the Baltic. The Rhine, the chief waterway of Germany, flows west from Lake Constance, turns north through a narrow and extremely fertile plain between the Black Forest and the Vosges, then turns westward at Mainz and passes through a picturesque gorge into the northern plain. The Ems and the Weser are entirely German from source to sea, and these, with the Elbe, discharge their waters into the North Sea. The Oder, almost entirely a German river, and the Vistula flow through great lagoons or "haffs" into the Baltic Sea. The Elbe, Vltava, Oder, Niemen, and Danube were created international waterways by the Treaty of Versailles.

Lakes are numerous in Germany, though none is of any great size. They occur chiefly in the Alpine region and in the northern plain. In the former region they are remnants of the Great Ice Age, and include Tegernsee and Königsee in the most southern portion of Germany. The lakes of the northern plain are very numerous and often of considerable depth. The Kurisches Haff is the largest of the German lakes, if the "haffs" are included with the inland lakes.

Climate and Rainfall.

There is not so much diversity of climate as might be expected from a hasty glance at the map. The cold of the northern plains is lessened by the presence of the sea, while the heat of the southern portion is modified by the altitude of that region. In general, however, Germany is not so favourably situated as France, for it is further north and further east, and the best climatic position in the south-west is mountainous. The most favourable climate is found in the

valley of the Middle Rhine and the valleys of the
Neckar, Main, and Moselle. The climate of Germany
becomes colder as we proceed from the south-west to
the north-east. The North Sea coast of Germany is
almost free from ice, while the Baltic Sea is usually
closed by ice for a portion of the year. In south
Germany the July temperature is above 70° F., and
the south-western plains of the Rhine have an annual
mean temperature of 50° F. The average rainfall for
the whole country is about 28 inches. As a rule the
rainfall decreases from west to east and from south to
north. The heaviest rainfall, of 40 inches per annum
or even more, is on the western or south-western slopes
of the mountains.

Plants and Animals.

Nearly one-half of Germany is under cultivation,
one fifth is pasture land, one-quarter is forest land, and
about one-twentieth is waste land. It will thus be
evident that the original plants and animals have a
very restricted area, and even the forests are no longer
in a state of nature, but are under systematic manage-
ment. The forests of north and central Germany
abound in small game and the wild boar is still sheltered.
In the Alps the chamois, the red deer, wild goat, fox,
and marten are found. Wolves are met with in Bavaria
and elsewhere, and in the plains of the north storks,
wild geese, and ducks are abundant. Both fresh and
salt water fish abound. No salmon are found in the
Danube, but this fish is plentiful in the North Sea and
Baltic rivers.

Agricultural Products.

Potatoes and rye, which form the chief food of the
people, are grown largely in the northern plain. Oats
and wheat are cultivated in Silesia, East Prussia, and
the Rhine provinces. The sugar-beet, the chief industrial plant, is most largely grown in Saxony and
Silesia, where sugar is manufactured. Flax is grown

in the same provinces and also along the Baltic. Hops
are grown mainly in the south, especially in Bavaria,
for the great breweries of Munich, the centre of the
German beer trade. The vine is cultivated for wine-

Vineyards on the bank of the Rhine.

making on the slopes of the Rhine valley, and the noted
Taunus wines are the produce of the hill slopes in the
vicinity of Wiesbaden. Fruit and tobacco are also
grown in the same regions. The raising of live-stock
is of the greatest importance in Germany. Horse-

breeding is chiefly confined to the plains of the north
and of the Alps.   Cattle are kept everywhere for beef
and for dairy purposes ; most sheep are raised in the
north of Prussia, but the finest wool is obtained in
Saxony ; and swine are kept principally in Westphalia.
Goats are less numerous than formerly, but they are
kept on the mountains for their milk.

Minerals.

Germany ranks next after Great Britain in the
value of its mineral production, and of the minerals,
coal and iron are the first in importance.   The most
extensive coal-fields are those of the Rühr valley in
Westphalia, of Upper Silesia, and of Saxony.   Lignite
is also abundant and furnishes fuel for various industries.   Iron ore is usually found in the same localities
as coal, thus fixing the sites of the great metal-working
and manufacturing towns.   Silver, copper, lead, and
tin are found in the Erzgebirge and the Harz districts,
zinc in Upper Silesia, and salt in Saxony, especially at
Stassfurt, where rock salt and potash salts are both produced.   Germany is the first silver-producing country
in Europe, and Upper Silesia has the largest output of
zinc in the world.

People and History.

The population of Germany has increased from
24,831,396 in 1816 to upwards of 59,000,000 at the
present time.   The average density to the square mile
is over 318 persons, while in Saxony, the most densely
populated State, it is over 805 persons.   In recent
years the average annual increase in the German
population is about 1·3 per cent. ; and the concentra-
tion of people in the great towns has not gone so
far as in some other countries.   The German-speaking
inhabitants number upwards of 52 millions ; there are
also Poles, besides Wends, Czechs, Lithuanians, Danes,
French, and Walloons.   The Germans are divided
into High and Low Germans.   High German is the

cultivated language of all the German states, while Low German is spoken mostly in the north and north-west.

In the earliest historic period, about fourth century B.C., the Germani were living between the Elbe and the Rhine and to the north of the Main. In succeeding centuries the Romans made their way into German territory only to be forced back by the Germans. The Holy Roman Empire was constituted in the ninth century, Charlemagne receiving the crown in 800, but under his successors France and Germany separated, and in 911 the Germans secured the right of electing their emperor. The ancient German Empire has been diminished by the loss of Switzerland, Belgium, and the Netherlands, and the present German Empire is entirely different from the Holy Roman Empire which came to an end in 1806. As a result of the Napoleonic Wars, the German Confederation was formed in 1815 lasting till 1866. In that year, as a result of the war between Austria and Prussia, the former country was separated from Germany, and later, in 1871, the new German Empire was constituted with the kings of Prussia as hereditary emperors. The re-annexation of Alsace-Lorraine followed the Franco-German War of 1870–71. From that period to 1914 the progress of the German Empire was remarkable. There was a steady increase in its commerce, a great development of its fleet, and an effort at colonial expansion, especially in Africa. It must not be forgotten that the Germans have a more systematic education than any other European nation. There are 21 universities, and the polytechnics and technical schools are very efficient. Perhaps the two outstanding facts in Germany's progress were the compulsory attendance at school of its children and the service in the army of every able-bodied young man. The Great War was disastrous to Germany, and according to the Treaty of Versailles she has agreed to cede Alsace-Lorraine to France, parts of West Prussia, Posen, and part of Upper Silesia to Poland, Moresnet, Eupen, and Malmédy to Belgium, and Memel and Danzig to the Allies; while the Saar Basin is placed under the League of Nations and North Sleswig has been restored to Denmark after a plebiscite.

With regard to religion, there is entire liberty of conscience, but the Jesuit order is interdicted in all parts of Germany. About 62 per cent. of the people are Protestants, and 36 per cent. Roman Catholics, who are in the majority in Bavaria and Baden. There are upwards of 600,000 Jews.

Industries and Manufactures.

Reference has already been made to the industries connected with agriculture, forestry, and mining, but besides these, all branches of manufacturing industry are vigorously carried on. Linen goods are made in Silesia, Westphalia, and Saxony, and cotton fabrics are produced in Rhenish Prussia and Saxony. The same districts, together with Pomerania, Bavaria, Würtemburg, and Baden, manufacture woollen goods. The silk industry centres in Düsseldorf, and jute-spinning is carried on at Brunswick, Meissen, and Bonn. Hosiery is made in Saxony and Thuringia, and thread in Saxony, Silesia, and the Rhine provinces. Wood-carving and the making of toys and wooden clocks flourish in Saxony, Bavaria, and the Black Forest. The glass factories of Silesia and Bavaria are important, and Saxony and Prussia produce excellent china and earthenware. Silver, gold, and jewellery work, as well as the manufacture of scientific and musical instruments, are associated with Augsburg, Nuremburg, Munich, and Berlin. The best iron and steel factories are in Silesia, Hanover, and Saxony, and printing and the allied arts are prominent in Munich and Leipzig. Beer is largely produced in Prussia and Bavaria; vinegar and oils in central and southern Germany; and beetroot, sugar, tobacco, and snuff in the northern cities of Germany. In the production of fine chemicals, dyes, and drugs, Germany is pre-eminent. Ships are built at Hamburg and at most of the Baltic ports.

Communications.

Besides about 8500 miles of waterways, Germany has a great railway system of over 36,000 miles, the greater part belonging to the state. Berlin is the centre of the railways and canals of the northern plain, and the railways are of international importance. The Orient express from Paris to Constantinople passes from Strassburg through Munich to Vienna; and the line from Cologne through Berlin to Warsaw unites France and Germany by the town of Samara on the Volga to the whole of eastern Asia. The most important lines in the south are those following the two banks of the Rhine from Cologne to Basel on the Swiss frontier, the outlet of the Westphalian manufacturing district, to Italy through Switzerland and the St Gothard tunnel. The construction of the great Alpine tunnels, the St Gothard and the Arlberg, in the west of Tirol, have had much influence on the increasing trade of Germany. There are 1500 miles of inland canals and 1600 miles of ship canals.

Commerce.

The enormous increase in German commerce with all parts of the world was one of the outstanding facts in the recent history of the country. The imports comprised grain and flour, raw wool, raw cotton, timber, yarns, coffee, hides, raw silk, horses, tobacco, coal, and petroleum, while the exports are sugar, woollen and cotton goods, coal, iron, machinery, and silk. The greatest import and export trade was with the United Kingdom, then with Austria-Hungary, Russia, and the United States. German trade policy was that of protection. For trading purposes, Germany was largely dependent on the ports of Belgium, Holland, France, Italy, and Austria, as there are few German seaports with a sufficient depth of water for the largest ships. All the Baltic ports are closed by ice in winter, and the navigable channels of the Elbe and the Weser are kept free by ice-breakers.

Government.

The German Empire that was formed in 1871 came
to an end on November 9, 1918, when the German
Emperor abdicated, and from that date Germany became a Republic.

Towns.

Berlin is the only town with nearly 3,800,000 people.
There are 40 other towns with over 100,000 and 36
towns between 50,000 and 100,000.

Berlin, on the Spree, is the seat of government.
It owes its large population mainly to the advantage
of its situation, for it is centrally situated in the
north German plain, and as a result railways and
other modern improvements have extended its natural
advantages. Its exchange is second only to that of
London. There are great engineering works, textile
industries, and immense breweries, while the manufacture of electrical apparatus and artistic metal-work
is a special feature. *Hamburg*, on the Elbe, 60 miles
from the sea, can be reached at high tide by the largest
steamers. It is the first trading-port on the continent,
its trade is highly organised, and the port includes that
of *Altona*. *Munich*, the capital of Bavaria, is an
important railway centre. It is famed for its art
galleries, and for its artistic manufactures in wood,
bronze, glass, and pottery. *Leipzig*, in Saxony, is the
chief centre of the German book trade, and its commerce
is yearly stimulated by fairs, when leather, furs, books,
and other goods are sold in enormous quantities.
Breslau, on the Oder, is the centre of a rich agricultural,
manufacturing, and mining district. *Dresden*, on the
Elbe, the capital of Saxony, has numerous manufactures,
especially porcelain and photographic materials. *Cologne*,
on the Rhine, owes its prosperity to the steamer traffic on
that river, and the frontier railway transport. *Frank-
fort-on-Main*, a river port of considerable importance
and one of the chief financial towns in Europe, con-

centrates the commerce of south-western Germany. *Nuremberg* (*Nürnberg*) has a fine commercial situation in Bavaria and has been famous for its manufactures

Berlin: the Victory Monument (1864—1871).

since the thirteenth century. It is now largely engaged in the manufacture of fine metal-work, dyes, pencils, and wooden toys. *Düsseldorf* has coal, iron, and

cotton industries and is the centre of the trade of the
Lower Rhine. *Essen* is the seat of Krupp's works,
famed for cast-steel goods and cannon. *Aachen* (*Aix-la-
Chapelle*) is engaged in woollen-weaving. *Stuttgart*, in
Würtemberg, is a railway centre and has an important
publishing trade. *Magdeburg*, on the Elbe, has extensive sugar refineries and is the centre of an industrial
district. *Chemnitz*, the German Manchester, has
large cotton factories and engineering works. *Bremen*
is a great tobacco market. It is the headquarters
of the North German Lloyd Steamship Company and
most of the German emigrants pass through it or
Hamburg. *Wilhelmshaven*, on the North Sea, and
Kiel, on the Baltic, are naval stations. *Stettin*, on the
Oder, the chief Baltic port, has ship-building works.
It is the nearest seaport to Berlin and the natural
outlet for the forest and mining products of Pomerania
and Silesia. *Danzig*, at the mouth of the Vistula, and
Königsberg, further east on the Pregel, are seaports
exporting oats, flax, rye, timber, and amber. By the
Treaty of Versailles Danzig and the surrounding country
was constituted a Free City under the League of Nations.
Danzig and Poland now form a single customs territory
with joint economic administration. The Free City has
an area of 709 square miles and a sea frontage of 35 miles.

Denmark.

Position and Extent.

Denmark consists of the low northward-pointing
peninsula of Jutland and the islands lying in the
Kattegat at the entrance to the Baltic. Including
the Faroe Islands the area of the kingdom of Denmark
is upwards of 17,144 square miles, and of this total the
peninsula of Jutland claims two-thirds. Denmark owes
its independence to the necessity felt by the Great
Powers that it should be kept as a neutral Power in case
of war. In 1864 its area was considerably diminished,
when Sleswig and Holstein became part of Prussia by

conquest; but North Sleswig was restored in 1919. Green-
land is now the only colonial possession of Denmark.
Since 1918 Iceland is united with Denmark only through
the identity of the Sovereign.

Surface and General Features.

Denmark, almost entirely surrounded by water, is
one of the most low-lying countries in Europe. The
North Sea coast is low, sandy, and regular, and behind
the sandy beaches and dunes there are large lagoons.
The Skaw, a long, narrow sand-spit, is the end of the
peninsula. The east coast is higher and more indented
and has some harbours for small ships. The islands
are hilly and have more variety of landscape, although
the highest point does not reach 600 feet. The Little
Belt, a channel between Jutland and Funen, is narrow
and difficult to navigate; the Great Belt, between
Funen and Seeland, is the only channel deep enough
for large war-vessels; and the Sound, between Seeland
and Sweden, rarely blocked by ice, is used chiefly by
merchant ships.

Climate and Productions.

It will be noted that Denmark has the same latitude
as Scotland south of Inverness, and its climate is similar
to that of the east of Scotland, except that it is somewhat warmer in summer and colder in winter. The
climate is generally less extreme than that of central
Europe, and although the channels often have drifting
ice, it is very rare indeed that they are closed for any
period.

No coal or metals are found in the country, but
peat is obtained from the moorlands of Jutland. The
people are enterprising and hard-working. The greater
portion gain their living by agriculture, and the remainder by manufactures, trade, fishing, or as sailors.
The forests of beech which formerly covered much of
the country have been cleared from extensive areas,
and these districts are now under pasture or growing

oats, barley, and rye. It will thus be evident that Denmark is essentially an agricultural country and devoted to the rearing of live-stock. Butter is the leading export and enormous quantities are exported to Great Britain. The other exports are barley, wheat-meal and flour, cattle, swine, and horses, and the chief imports are manufactured articles, coffee, sugar, and tobacco.

People and History.

The population is about 3 millions, of whom the larger portion live on the Baltic Islands. The people belong to the Norse branch of the Teutonic family, and their power once extended over Norway, south Sweden, and England. They lost south Sweden in the seventeenth century; Norway in 1814; and the two provinces of Sleswig-Holstein in 1864. The Danes belong to the Lutheran church, and are ruled by a limited monarchy and two houses of parliament.

Administration and Communications.

The country is divided into seven districts for administrative purposes. Roads are good and the railway system is very complete. Most of the lines are owned by the state, and through carriages are ferried across arms of the sea in steamers. There are good canals ; the Agger canal connects Liim Fjord with the Kattegat. Although the Liim Fjord bisects the peninsula, it is not useful for shipping on account of its shallowness.

Towns.

Copenhagen, on the Sound, is the capital and the only really good harbour. It is strongly fortified and has many good public buildings, including the royal palace and the university. *Aarhus* is the largest town in Jutland. *Esbjerg*, on the North Sea, has a growing trade with Harwich. *Elsinore*, a fortified port at the north of the Sound, till 1857 collected passage dues from ships using that channel. The passage is now free, Denmark having received £3,500,000 as compensation.

Scandinavia.

Position and Extent.

Norway and Sweden together form Scandinavia, a great peninsula in the north-west of Europe. Norway, which forms the western and smaller portion, is somewhat larger than the British Isles, and Sweden in the east has an area equal to twice that of Great Britain. The length of the peninsula is 1160 miles and the breadth varies from 230 to 470 miles.

A fjord in Norway.

Surface and General Features.

The surface of this peninsula may be described as a high tableland varying from about 1000 feet in the north to 3000 feet in the south. Throughout its extent this tableland presents a generally desolate aspect, and the prevailing vegetation consists of heaths, mosses, and lichens. Norway has the largest proportion of

B.   11 this tableland, as the lowlands of the peninsula are mainly in the east and south. On the western side this high, barren plateau is penetrated by fjords and fringed by numerous islands, including the Lofoten group. To the eastward the plateau sinks in terraces to a plain along the Gulf of Bothnia. The great mountain groups consist of the Kiolen Mountains, and the Hardanger, Sogne, and Dovre Fjelds. Norway is one of the most mountainous countries in Europe, and the highest peak is Galdhöpiggen (8400 feet). Many snowfields and glaciers are formed, especially in the north and towards the west coast, and from Jostedals-brae, the largest of the snowfield districts, no less than 24 glaciers flow.

The broken and indented nature of the coast has already been mentioned, and between the islands there are tremendous currents, such as the famous Maelström, whose force has been much exaggerated. The off-lying islands along the Norwegian coast afford excellent harbours for the fishermen. The Swedish coast is low and sandy, and has the large islands of Gothland and Oland in the Baltic.

Rivers and Lakes.

The rivers are generally so much obstructed by rapids as to be of little use for navigation. It will be seen that the rivers on the eastern side are the longer, and the only important river in Norway is the Glommen. Although the rivers are not of much use for navigation, the lakes in the lowland region of Sweden are of great importance. The four great lakes are Vener, Vetter, Hjelmar, and Mälar; and Vener and Vetter together with a part of the Göta River are all connected by a ship canal, so that there is direct water communication between the opposite coasts of Sweden.

Climate and Rainfall.

Owing to the great range of its latitude there is considerable difference between the temperature of the north and south, and the west has a milder climate than the east because of the prevailing westerly winds. Sweden is more exposed to continental conditions, but the higher parts of Norway have a very severe climate. The greatest cold is experienced in the northern portion of the interior of Sweden. In Stockholm the average temperature ranges from 28·5° F. in January, the coldest month, to 60·3° F. in June, the warmest month. The Norwegian coast has the greatest rainfall and there also fog is prevalent in the winter, although there is comparatively little snow. At Dombesten the rainfall is 79 inches and at Christiania 28 inches. Sweden has its highest rainfall on the west coast, and in the vicinity of the Kattegat 35 inches are recorded. Most of Scandinavia is covered with snow in the winter and the seaports of Sweden are then closed with ice.

Productions and Industries.

The chief production is timber, and the manufacture of wood-pulp for paper-making and of lucifer matches are important industries. Sweden grows oats and barley, and makes increasing quantities of butter, but Norway has practically no agriculture. Norway derives much of its riches from the sea, and cod, herrings, and train-oil, a product of the whale-fisheries, are of considerable value. Both countries suffer from a lack of coal, but the iron mines of Dannemora have made Sweden famous for its iron for a long period. Sweden also produces copper, silver, and lead. Cattle-breeding is of some importance in Sweden, and in the north reindeer are reared. The manufactures of Sweden include those connected with iron-works, chemical works, wood-working factories, lucifer-match factories, breweries, and distilleries. In Norway the main resources of the people are the fisheries, the forests, and the shipping. Ship-building has always been an important industry, and the Norwegian mercantile marine is large, for Norway does a great carrying trade for other nations, especially in sailing-ships.

People and History.

The bulk of the people belong to the Scandinavian branch of the Teutonic race. In the early centuries Norway, Sweden, and Denmark were united, but Norway has formed a separate kingdom since 872 and in the same century Sweden had its own king. Sweden became the most powerful country of the north from 1537 to 1660, especially under the great leadership of Gustavus Adolphus. After many vicissitudes the French Marshal, Bernadotte, became king of Sweden in 1818, and eventually of both kingdoms. This union continued till 1905, when it was decided that Norway should once again have its own king. The Norwegians chose their king from the Danish royal house, while the Swedes retained their old king. The population in both kingdoms is about 8 millions, but Sweden has more than twice as many people as Norway, which has only 18 persons to the square mile. The people, honest, thrifty, and hard-working, are members of the Lutheran church, which was established in the sixteenth century.

Administration and Communications.

Each country has its own king and two houses of parliament. Sweden is divided into Sveland, Götaland, and Norrland, and Norway into the northern, southern, and western districts. Along the Norwegian coast communication is kept up by steamers all the year, and several lines of steamers run between Norway and Britain. The Norwegian roads are good, and three railway lines join Norway with Sweden. Sweden has a splendid system of roads over the country, and its railway communications have been so much improved that its railway mileage is the greatest in Europe in proportion to the number of its inhabitants.

Towns in Norway.

Nearly all the Norwegian towns of importance are seaports. *Christiania*, the capital, is on a fjord at the head of the Skagerrak. It is the chief harbour and the only industrial town. *Stavanger* and *Bergen* are the headquarters of the fisheries, and *Trondhjem* has a good harbour. *Drammen* has trade in logs and wood-pulp, and *Hammerfest*, the most northerly town in Europe, is a centre for whale-fishing.

In Sweden.

Stockholm, the capital, stands at the Baltic entrance of Lake Mälar and is the chief industrial town of the country. It has a fine harbour, and, besides the royal palace, there are many good public buildings. *Upsala* has an ancient cathedral and its university dates from the fifteenth century. *Göteborg*, on the Skagerrak, is the chief port for Swedish exports. *Falun* has great copper works. *Norrköpping* is a flourishing industrial centre. *Malmo* and *Helsingborg*, on the Sound, are two progressive seaports.

Russia.

Position and Extent.

Russia, which occupies the whole of eastern Europe, has an area of nearly two million square miles, or more than half that of the entire continent.

Surface and General Features.

The greater portion of the surface consists of a vast plain 700 miles wide, which crosses it from south-west to north-east and connects the elevated plains of central Europe with the Urals. The Valdai Hills rise to 1100 feet, and the Urals, which consist of parallel ridges running south-west to north-east, have summits upwards of 5000 feet high. The Caucasus Mountains in the south are of great importance and have the highest peaks in Europe, Mount Elbruz reaching 18,256 feet.

The rivers of Russia are numerous and long, the

majority of them being navigable nearly to their sources
and many of them for a great distance by steamers.
Of course they are all more or less subject to the draw-
back of ice, for no Russian river port is open for more
than 10 months in the year.   The chief rivers rise in
the north-west of the plateau ; some of them flow
north-west while the others go south-east.   There are
about 50,000 miles of navigable rivers in Russia and
about 500 miles of canal, but the system of the Neva
and the Volga carries two-thirds of the European trade.
It includes Lakes Ladoga and Onega with access to the
Baltic Sea, the river Dwina entering the White Sea,
and the Volga, 2200 miles long, with its lengthy
tributaries flowing to the Caspian.   At Tsaritsin the
Volga approaches within 50 miles the Don, to which
barges are transferred by railway and floated down to
the Baltic Sea.   Another system links the Baltic
through the Vistula and Dnieper with the Black Sea
and Mediterranean.

Climate and Rainfall.

With the exception of the Baltic provinces, the south
of the Crimea, and a tract along the Black Sea, the
climate is continental.   The winters are generally long
and cold ; the summers are short and hot.   All over
Russia the winter temperature of January is below
freezing-point, varying from 22° F. in the west to 5° in
the east.   All the rivers are frozen over in December,
and they remain under ice for about 100 days in the
south and 160 days in the north.   In summer the
Russian temperature is high and reaches 78° at Astrakhan.   The rainfall all over Russia is generally small,
and about half the entire area in the north-east, east,
and south-east has a yearly rainfall of less than 20
inches.

Productions.

It is estimated that not more than one-quarter of
the surface of Russia is arable, and from the preceding

paragraph it will be gathered that the climate in the north and south-east puts a limit to cultivation in these regions. In the north the tundra region has mosses, lichens, and shrubs. This is succeeded by the forest region of coniferous and deciduous trees. The "steppes" are immense plains covered with grass and devoid of trees. The "black earth region," in southern Russia, has a fertile soil and grows the greatest quantity of the Russian corn crops. The chief of the grain crops is, however, rye, which is grown to an amount four times as great as wheat. Oats are largely produced; and flax and hemp in the Baltic provinces and Poland, and sugar beet in the south, are important crops. The Russian forests, the largest wooded area in Europe, are under government control. Horses, cattle, and sheep are pastured on the steppes in spring and autumn. The woods abound with fur-bearing animals, such as the squirrel, and the great rivers swarm with fish.

Minerals.

The mineral wealth of Russia is enormous and both coal and iron are abundant. Coal is found near the Sea of Azov, in the valley of the Donetz, a district which yields the largest and best supply. The Ural Mountains, the great mineral region, yield coal, iron, gold, zinc, silver, and platinum. There are rock-salt mines in several places, and salt works among the saline lakes of the steppes. The western shore of the Caspian has some very productive petroleum wells, particularly at Baku.

Industries, Trade, and Commerce.

Agriculture is the chief occupation of the Russians, and only in parts of central Russia does manufacturing industry rank in importance. The chief industrial centres are Moscow and Petrograd. The woollen trade is growing in the south, and the production of alcohol, especially *vodka*, the national spirit, is enormous. There are numerous sugar mills and tallow factories in Russia;

but the domestic industries carried on in the homes of
the peasants are of greater importance than elsewhere
in Europe. The trade of Russia is mainly with Germany
and Great Britain. The exports are chiefly wheat from
the Black Sea, oats and rye from the Baltic ports,
timber, flax, hemp, cattle and their products, and petroleum. The chief imports are raw materials for the
increasing manufactures, coal, tea, and manufactured
articles. The importance of the Russian rivers in the
trade has already been mentioned, and the railways,
radiating from Moscow, extend to 35,000 miles. The
Siberian railway to Vladivostok on the Pacific was
completed in 1904.

People and History.

The population of Russia, which is rapidly increasing,
is about 131,000,000. There is a great variety of nation-
alities, but the majority of the people are Russian
Slavs. Jews are numerous in west Russia and there
are Armenians, Kurds, and Persians in the Caucasus.
Besides these there are Tartars and Kalmucks in the
Caucasus, and many Germans in the Baltic provinces
and the chief towns.

Most of the people belong to the Greek Church,
officially styled the Orthodox Catholic Church.

In the Middle Ages, the country suffered from the
Mongol invasion, and it was not till Ivan the Great
(1462–1505) had expelled these terrible invaders that
Russia began to develop. Then it was that Moscow
became the capital of an important state which was
soon to reach from the White Sea to the Black Sea.
Under Peter the Great (1689–1725) Russia became
dominant on the Baltic, and under Catherine II great
additions were made to Russia at the expense of Poland,
Turkey, and Sweden. In the nineteenth century
Russian extensions of territory were made in Asia,
but the defeat in 1904–5 of Russia by Japan, both on
land and sea, put a limit to Russian aggression for a
time.

Moscow.

Administration.

Russia took part in the Great War of 1914–18 with Britain and France as her allies. In 1917, owing to a revolution, the Emperor Nicholas II abdicated. Poland and Finland in the same year secured their independence as sovereign states, and later, various other districts have received formal recognition, viz. Latvia, Lithuania, Esthonia.

The greater part of the former Russian Empire is now a republic under the rule of the Bolsheviks.

Towns.

Petrograd (formerly St Petersburg), the capital, has been accessible to large ships only since 1885; before that date Kronstadt was its port. It has wide streets and splendid buildings, and is the great centre of trade and industry. *Moscow*, the former capital and still in some respects the chief city, is the chief railway centre, the first manufacturing town for textiles, metal work and paper, and the centre of inland trade. *Kieff*, on the Dnieper, has important fairs and beet-sugar works. *Kharkoff*, on the northern border of the steppes and in the heart of the black earth region, has a large horse trade. *Kazan* and *Saratov*, on the Volga, with tobacco and salt works, have a large shipping trade. *Nizhni-Novgorod*, at the confluence of the Oka and Volga, has great annual fairs visited by tens of thousands of merchants with goods brought from all parts of Europe and Asia. *Reval* and *Riga*, ports on the Baltic, trade largely in oats, rye, wood, hemp, flax, and tallow. *Odessa*, the busiest port on the Black Sea, is the chief grain port of Russia and the seat of the Russian Steam Navigation Company. The other seaports on the Black Sea or the Sea of Azov are *Taganrog*, *Kherson*, and *Nicolaeff*. *Sebastopol*, in the Crimea, is now a naval port and closed to trade. *Archangel*, on the White Sea, exports flax, timber, tar, and tallow.

Astrakhan, on the Caspian Sea, has sturgeon fisheries, and trades with *Baku*, the great oil town.

Finland.

Position, Area, and Surface.

Finland is situated between the Gulf of Bothnia on the west and Russia on the east, and between Lapland on the north and the Gulf of Finland on the south. Its area is 150,000 square miles, and of this area about 11 per cent. is under lakes.

Productions and Industry.

Agriculture is the chief occupation of the people, although only one-twelfth of the land is under cultivation. The chief crops are rye, barley, oats, potatoes, flax, hemp, and hay. The production of butter is an important industry. The domestic animals are horses, horned cattle, sheep, and pigs.

More than half Finland is covered with forests of pine and spruce, and lumbering is the chief industry. Iron, copper, and sulphur are found, but not in large quantities. The chief manufactures are those connected with iron, textiles, wool, paper, leather, chemicals, and brewing.

Trade and Commerce.

The foreign trade is chiefly with Russia, Sweden, Norway, Denmark, Germany, and Great Britain. The principal exports are paper, timber, butter, iron and iron goods, textiles, leather, and hides: the chief imports are cereals, coffee, sugar, fish, cotton, and machinery.

For internal communication Finland has a remarkable system of lakes, which are connected with each other and with the Gulf of Finland by canals.

People and History.

The population is about 3½ millions, and the chief religions are Lutheran, Greek Church, and Roman Catholic.

Finland was joined to the Russian Empire as a Grand Duchy in 1809; in 1917 it declared itself an independent and Sovereign State; and in 1919 it became a Republic.

Towns.

Helsingfors is the capital and largest town. It is a busy seaport and its university is an important scientific centre. *Abo* is the most ancient town in Finland. Its chief trade is in timber and grain. *Viborg* is the most frequented harbour of Finland and ranks second in the value of its trade.

Austria and Hungary.

Position and Extent.

Austria and Hungary are two states in the middle of Europe. The area is over 65,000 square miles. As a result of the Great War these two countries were reduced from their previous area of 240,000 square miles, and various portions were annexed to Czecho-Slovakia, Rumania, Yugo-Slavia, and Italy.

Surface and General Character.

The greater part of this geographical territory is mountainous or hilly. The great mountain chains are the Alps and the Karpathians. The Alps, stretching from Switzerland to the Danube, have the highest peaks in Austria—Ortler Spitze (12,814 feet) and Gross Glockner (12,400 feet). The Karpathians, sweeping in a semicircular form, culminate in peaks 8000 to 8500 feet.

The larger portions of Austria and Hungary belong to the middle basin of the Danube, which is navigable for steamers throughout its whole course in these countries. Navigation, formerly impeded by the rapids at the Iron Gate, was rendered free in 1896, when a permanent channel, 10 feet in depth, was completed. The chief affluents of the Danube are the Inn, Save, Drave, March, Waag, and Theiss. The last river drains nearly half of Hungary. The other rivers are the Vistula, Elbe, and Dniester.

There are some beautiful lakes in Tirol, but the largest lakes are in Hungary—notably Balaton and Neusiedler See. Zirknitz Lake is in Illyria.

Climate.

Owing to its land-locked position, the country has a climate which is generally continental, but on account of its extent and the variety of its surface there are considerable variations. Throughout the country the summers are hot and the winters very cold. The rainfall is low over the Hungarian plain, ranging from 20 to 25 inches, and is heaviest in Tirol and around the Karpathians and the Alps, where it reaches 40 to 50 inches. In Hungary the *Fata Morgana*, a mirage which rises about noon and spreads over the heated plain as far as one can see, is sometimes visible in the summer. The Alpine provinces have the *föhn*, a prevalent warm south wind.

Productions and Resources.

The extensive forests yield large supplies of timber, and agriculture employs two-thirds of the people. Wheat is largely raised, especially in Hungary, but oats, barley, maize, and rye also are widely grown. Sugar-beet is grown in Austria and Hungary, which are also famous for hops. Vine culture is carried on, and some of the wines, such as Tokay and Karlowitz, are of European renown. Tobacco, flax, and hemp are other products that occupy considerable areas.

Austria is rich in minerals. There are gold and silver mines in Hungary, and quicksilver is obtained from Idria in Carniola. Coal and iron are both plentiful, but they are found wide apart, so that the yield of the latter is not so great as it might be. Some copper, zinc, and lead are also produced.

Industries, Trade, and Commerce.

Agriculture is the main occupation of both countries; but mining gives employment to large numbers. Piano-making and the manufacture of motor-cars and textiles are of much importance in Austria.

By far the larger part of the trade before the Great War was done by rail with Germany, and the next best markets were Rumania, Russia, Italy, and Serbia. The trade with Great Britain was relatively small. The chief exports were grain, sugar, eggs, timber, minerals, and glass-ware, and the imports included raw wool, cotton, coal and coke, tobacco, leather, silk, and coffee.

Vienna is the centre whence trade routes and railways radiate. The chief Austrian tunnels through the Alps are the Brenner, Semmering, and Arlberg. The Brenner tunnel serves as the direct route between Bohemia and Italy; the Arlberg tunnel is the shortest route between Vienna and Switzerland; and the Semmering tunnel is the shortest route between Italy and Vienna.

People and History.

The population is about 20 million, there being 6 million in Austria and 14 million in Hungary. This population is very unevenly distributed, being generally sparse in the Alpine and Karpathian districts and populous in the south-west and north-west. With the exception of Russia, Austria has more distinct races than any other European country. The Slavs are the most numerous and form about 40 per cent. of the whole population. The Germans number about 25 per cent., and there are representatives of the Romance peoples, Italians, Rumanians, and others. The Magyars, who live chiefly in Hungary, form 16 per cent. of the population. The remainder comprise Jews, Armenians, and gipsies. The chief languages spoken are German, Hungarian, and Polish; and the bulk of the people are Roman Catholics, but there are many belonging to the Greek Church, besides Armenians, Lutherans, and Jews.

The history of Austria is of deep interest. The Romans pushed their empire to the south-west of this country but not much beyond the Danube. In the ninth century Charlemagne extended his empire as far east as Austria, and the name *Oestervick* first appears in 896. After coming into the possession of the House of Hapsburg it rose to be a powerful state in the thirteenth century, and the princes of that family extended their dominion by the inclusion of Bohemia, Hungary, and other states; so that down to the nineteenth century they held the throne of the Holy Roman Empire or German Empire. After the Austro-Prussian war of 1866 Austria was separated from Germany, and in the following year Austria-Hungary was re-constituted on a dual basis. In 1878 Bosnia and Herzegovina were occupied, and in 1908 they were annexed to the Empire.

Administration.

On October 31, 1918, Hungary declared itself independent of Austria and in the following month was proclaimed an independent Republic. Austria was proclaimed a Republic on November 12, 1918.

Towns.

Vienna, the capital of Austria, with 2,000,000 people, owes much of its importance to its position, for it is situated where all the western trade of Hungary converges on the narrower part of the Danube valley. It has a famous exchange, and great cotton, silk, and woollen factories, besides breweries and an extensive wine trade. *Budapest*, a double town, the capital of Hungary, has a central position on a plain and is thus well placed for trade, especially in grain, cattle, and wine. *Gratz* is the centre of the Styrian iron trade.

Poland.

Position, Area, and Surface.

Poland is an inland state having Germany on the west, Russia on the east, and Czecho-Slovakia on the south. The surface is generally flat and uninteresting, and the country is watered by the river Vistula. The area is approximately 149,000 square miles.

Productions and Industry.

About 85 per cent. of Poland is productive, and of this area about one-quarter is forest. The remainder is arable, meadow, and pasture. The chief crops are wheat, rye, barley, oats, potatoes, and beetroot. The domestic animals are horses, cattle, sheep, and swine.

The most important industries are those connected with textiles, food, metals, and mines. Before the Great War there were extensive sugar refineries and distilleries. The chief minerals are coal, iron, zinc, lead, salt, and rock-oil. It is said that Galicia produces 5 per cent. of the total petroleum of the world.

Trade and Commerce.

The exports were chiefly manufactured goods, furniture, woollen and cotton goods, and alcoholic beverages which went to Russia; and the imports were raw wool and cotton, jute, cutlery, tools, and machinery. Since the Great War this State is quickly recovering and has 7295 miles of railway open for traffic, while there are 1875 miles of navigable waterways.

People and History.

Until the end of the eighteenth century Poland was an independent state, and in the fifteenth century it was one of the most highly civilised nations in Europe. In the seventeenth century Poland declined, and in

1772, 1793, and 1795 it was divided among Prussia, Russia, and Austria. In 1807 Napoleon formed it into a State under the title of the Duchy of Warsaw, but in 1815 this was altered and Poland was re-partitioned as before.

During the Great War the country was invaded by Germany and suffered all the horrors of that conflict. In 1918 Poland declared its independence, which was acknowledged at Versailles in 1919.

Warsaw.

The population is estimated at 27,000,000, or a density of 180 per square mile. The great majority of the people profess the Roman Catholic faith, but there is no State Church in Poland.

Towns.

Warsaw is the capital and the point of convergence of commercial routes from all parts of Russia and Western Europe. It has the ancient palace of the Kings of Poland, and a university. *Lodz* is the second city in population and industry. *Krakow* was once the capital of Poland; it has considerable trade and is one of the chief centres of Polish life. *Lwow* (Lemberg), the third Polish town in point of population, is the seat of a university.

Czecho-Slovakia.

Position, Size, and Surface.

This inland country is between Germany and Poland on the north and Austria and Hungary on the south. The area is estimated at 54,000 square miles. This State consists of Bohemia, Moravia, Silesia, Slovakia, and Ruthenia, and some smaller territories assigned to it by the Peace Conference of 1919. Bohemia is in the upper Elbe basin and has mountains on three sides: on the south-west the Bohemian forest, which rises to nearly 5000 feet; on the north-west the Erzgebirge, which has heights of over 4000 feet; and in the north-east the Riesengebirge, which rises to 5300 feet. The south-east of Bohemia is without a distinct range of mountains, and the interior is hilly in the south and a level lowland in the north. Moravia and Silesia stretch over the lowlands bordering the western chains of the Karpathians. The south is drained by the March to the Danube and the north by the Oder to the Baltic Sea.

Climate.

In the lowlands of the interior the climate is pleasant—the summer is warm and the winter not too cold. In the south the climate is more severe, especially on the surrounding mountains. The rainfall is moderate, and a good deal of snow falls in the winter.

Productions and Industry.

Bohemia is very productive. Wheat, beetroot, vine, and hops are extensively grown, besides rye, oats, and potatoes in the hilly regions. Extensive forests cover the mountains of the interior and of the border land. The mineral wealth of Bohemia now consists in its coal, for most of its mines of precious metals are exhausted. Lignite is found in large quantities; there are iron mines in the middle; and the quartz of the sandstone mountains is the source of the glass manufacture of Bohemia.

In Silesia and Moravia barley and beetroot are largely grown and the vine is cultivated. The Karpathians are extensively wooded. The Siberian coal-field causes the iron industry in its neighbourhood to flourish.

In Bohemia there are cotton and woollen manufactures; paper is made from the wood of the forest district; sugar is extensively produced from the beetroot; and beer is brewed at Pilsen.

People and History.

The population is about 14 millions and consists of Czechs, Slovaks, Magyars, and Germans. Bohemia is densely populated, having above 315 to the square mile, and in the industrial centres of Moravia and Silesia the density is equally great. The majority of the people are Roman Catholics, but there are many belonging to the Greek Church, besides a large number of Protestants and Jews.

The Czecho-Slovak State came into existence in 1918, and the National Assembly, which met at Prague, took over the government of the Czecho-Slovak countries which had formerly belonged to Austria-Hungary, and declared the new state to be a Republic.

Towns.

Prague, the capital, on both sides of the Moldau, has a population of over 600,000. It has considerable trade, largely owing to its position. *Brno*, in Moravia, has woollen manufactures. *Olmütz* was the former capital of Moravia. *Troppau* is the capital of Silesia.

Rumania.

Position and Extent.

Rumania is a kingdom lying in the lower basin of the Danube and bounded by Russia, Hungary, the Black Sea, and Bulgaria. It consists of the two old principalities of Moldavia and Walachia, and of Bessarabia, Bukovina, Transylvania, and three smaller divisions. The entire area is 122,282 square miles.

Surface, Climate, and Productions.

Rumania has been described as an irregular inclined plain, sloping down from the Karpathians (3000 to 9000 feet high) to the northern bank of the Danube. The country is traversed by numerous water-courses, some of which are dry in summer. The mouth of the Danube is divided into numerous branches, of which the most important are those of Kilia, Sulina, and St George. On the lower Danube great improvements have been effected in recent years, and the Sulina mouth has been straightened and deepened, so that large vessels can ascend to Braila. The navigation of the Danube is free to foreign vessels of any nationality by international treaty.

The climate of Rumania is similar to that of the Russian steppes, having hot summers and cold winters. The rainfall is nowhere heavy, and the mean temperature for the year at Bukharest is 51° F.

South-eastern Walachia and the Dobruja are mainly pastoral districts. The Rumanian plain is very fertile, and wheat and all kinds of grain are grown in abundance. Agriculture is the one great industry, and grain forms the bulk of the exports. The Karpathians are well wooded and there cattle-rearing and forestry are of importance, while on the lower slopes there is much cultivation of fruit.

People, History, and Industries.

The population of about 17 millions is largely composed of Orthodox Greek Christians, but there are many Roman Catholics, Protestants, and Jews. The Rumanians are descended from the original inhabitants, the Dacians, who came under the Roman rule—hence the name of the country. Out of several small states, Moldavia and Walachia became dominant, but they eventually came under the yoke of Turkey. Owing to Russian influence, and as a result of the Berlin Treaty of 1878, Rumania obtained its independence, giving Bessarabia to Russia in return for the Dobruja. In 1881 it was declared a hereditary kingdom with two houses of parliament. As a result of the Great War, Rumania was much enlarged.

The industries include flour- and saw-milling, match-making, brewing, distilling, tanning, and leather-work. The peasants have home industries, spinning, weaving, and dyeing fabrics for their own garments. As already mentioned, the people live mainly by agriculture, but there are industries connected with salt-mining and the extraction of petroleum, which is largely exported.

Towns.

Bukharest, originally the chief town of Walachia, is now the capital of the kingdom. It is the intellectual centre of Rumania and has a very large trade. *Jassy*, near the Pruth, is the provincial capital of Moldavia. *Galatz* and *Braila* are the principal commercial towns on the lower Danube and export grain chiefly in British ships.

The Balkan Peninsula.

Position and Extent.

The Balkan Peninsula comprises the greater portion of the region to the south of the Danube. Including the adjacent islands, Crete, the Ionian Islands, and the Aegean Islands, the area of the various states—European Turkey, Greece, Bulgaria, Serb, Croat, and Slovene State, and Albania—is about 250,000 square miles. The long and narrow Dardanelles and the Bosporus separate it from Asia, and the wider Strait of Otranto from Italy. It will be noted that the Balkan is the most easterly of the three peninsulas stretching south from the European mainland, and that it terminates in Cape Matapan.

Surface and General Features.

The Balkan Peninsula is rugged and mountainous; it is penetrated from the north by the Balkan range and the Dinaric Alps, the former in the north-east and the latter in the west. The Balkan range is a continuation of the Karpathians and in parts rises to 7800 feet. The Dinaric Mountains, a continuation of the Alps, consist of parallel chains running parallel to the coast through Montenegro and Albania into Greece, and rising to 6500 feet. What is known as the Thraco-Macedonian region extends between the two mountain ranges and forms the nucleus of the peninsula. The mountainous Rhodope district reaches a height of nearly 10,000 feet; Shardagh, in Upper Macedonia, is the highest peak in the peninsula, being just over 10,000 feet above sea level.

The river valleys of the Morava, Vardar, and Maritza are narrow but very fertile, and have long been the centres of cultivation and the main lines of communication. The Danube is an international highway from its mouth in the Black Sea for more than 500 miles westward. It is under the control of a commission and is kept open for ocean-going steamers by engineering works at the Sulina mouth, the other two outlets not being accessible to large ships. As a rule, the river is closed to sea trade by ice for the first two months of the year.

Climate and Productions.

The peninsular character of this region and its southerly latitude are counterbalanced by the easterly position, which renders the climate one of extremes. This is more particularly the case in the north, where it is continental, but to the south it is warmer and of the Mediterranean type. The rainfall is heaviest on the western side of the peninsula, and is less on the east coast than in the interior. The rainfall on the Adriatic shores is heavy throughout the year, but especially in autumn.

Among the wild animals, the wolf and the bear are found on the mountains, the jackal on the southern plains, and buffaloes and oriental fat-tailed sheep are common. Along the west coast there is the typical Mediterranean vegetation such as evergreen shrubs, olives, figs, oranges, and lemons; this is poorly developed in the south and lacking in the interior, while in the east there are steppes. The chief commercial products of the peninsula are nearly all agricultural; cereals are grown in Bulgaria, Eastern Rumelia, and Turkey; currants in Greece; and wine, tobacco, and silk are produced almost everywhere. Orchards abound in Serbia, and dried plums (prunes) are largely exported. The cultivation of roses is noteworthy, as this pursuit is for the sake of producing attar of roses, a valuable perfume.

The Balkan Peninsula is rich in minerals, but owing to the apathy of the people and the defective communication these are very meagrely developed. Greece is the only country where mineral products are largely exported. Silver, lead, iron ore, and the statuary marble of the island of Paros form about one-fifth of the value of the exports of Greece. Serbia produces silver, lead, copper, and coal, and the Rhodope Mountains yield copper. Salt is obtained on the shores of the Adriatic and the Aegean.

Communications and Industries.

As before noted, the Danube is the line of communication in the north; the other rivers are of little importance for trade, and the rugged character of the surface hinders the construction of roads and railways. In recent years, railways from Belgrade along the Varada, Morava, and Maritza valleys have been constructed, and in 1879 a carriage road was made over the Balkans at the Shipka Pass (4000 feet).

The Isthmus of Corinth has been pierced by a ship-canal, 26 feet deep, which enables vessels not only to save time, but also to avoid the dangerous voyage through the rocky waters in the vicinity of Cerigo.

Agriculture, on the plains and in the valleys, and rearing live-stock are the chief industries. The manufactures are almost entirely of local importance; the making of carpets, chiefly at Adrianople and Salonika, is the only branch of manufacturing industry that gives an export of any value. The Greeks have always been famous sailors and they do most of the trade of the peninsula. The chief countries having trade with the Balkan Peninsula are the United Kingdom, Italy, and France.

People and History.

The Balkan Peninsula was originally occupied by the Thracians, the Illyrians, and the Macedonians. The Greeks spread over the south-east of the peninsula, and later, under Roman and Byzantine rule, the whole region flourished. Constantinople, the capital of the eastern Roman Empire, was the most famous city in the world for trade and industry. The Slavs, consisting mainly of Serbians in the west and Bulgarians in the east, drove back the Greeks, Romans, and Illyrians to the south and south-west. The Slavs became Christians in the ninth century, but their supremacy was terminated by the invasion of the Turks in 1453 when the Byzantine Empire fell. The heavy yoke of the Turks put an end to the prosperity of the Peninsula till the latter part of the nineteenth century, when the Turko-Russian War in 1878 was followed by the Treaty of Berlin and the Balkan Peninsula was divided into five states—Turkey, Bulgaria, Serbia,

Montenegro, and Bosnia and Herzegovina. The latter were eventually annexed to Austria in 1908, and, as a result of the war between Turkey and the other Balkan States in 1912–13, the Turkish territory was reduced to a small area lying east of a line drawn from Enos on the Aegean Sea to Midia on the Black Sea. As a result of the Great War, Turkish territory was further reduced, and Serbia was enlarged by additions from Austria-Hungary and Bulgaria. The latter state was also deprived of its Aegean littoral.

The Geographical Character of Greece.

The land now called Greece by us has always been known to its own people as Hellas. It is a land of islands and peninsulas, and so it was the first part of Europe to stand forth as great and free in the history of the world; for it must be remembered that, in early times, it was always the sea coast which was first civilised, because it was the part which could most easily have trade with other parts of the world. As Greece was the first part of Europe to become civilised, so its coasts and islands were earlier and more highly civilised than the inland parts, which are almost everywhere full of mountains and valleys. Each valley or island or little peninsula had its own town, with its own little territory, forming a separate government and having the right of making war and peace, just as if it had been a great kingdom. Thus it was that the geographical nature of the land settled the history of the Greek people, and Greek merchants and sailors spread the culture of their people by founding colonies in every part of the world then known. The change of trade-routes, the inroads of barbaric tribes, and the tyranny of the Turks brought about the ruin of the land. The present kingdom of Greece is due to the war of independence from 1821 to 1829. The Ionian Islands were ceded by Great Britain in 1864, and the Treaty of Berlin extended its territory to the north. As a result of the war with Turkey in 1912–13, Greece received a further accession of territory on the mainland and by the cession of Crete, and at the end of the Great War Thrace was ceded to Greece by Bulgaria.

Towns.

Constantinople, on the Golden Horn, commands the Bosporus, the narrow outlet of the Black Sea into the Sea of Marmora. It is the centre of the Turkish Empire and a commercial city with a large foreign population in the suburbs of Pera and Galata. *Salonika*, on the Aegean, is an outlet for the silk-growing villages of the west and is in railway communication with western Europe. *Adrianople*, on the Maritza, has carpet factories and distilleries of attar of roses. It is a place of great military importance. *Gallipoli*, at the inner end of the Dardanelles is a naval port. *Athens*, on the Gulf of Aegina, is the capital of Greece. It is the only large town, and has *Piraeus* for its port. *Patras*, on the Gulf of Corinth is joined by a railway to Athens. *Belgrade*, the capital of Serb, Croat, and Slovene State, is at the junction of the Save and Danube and exports grain down the Danube. *Sofia*, the capital of Bulgaria, is at an important meeting-place of roads. It is an ancient town, but has been completely rebuilt. *Rustchuk*, *Vidin*, *Silistria*, and *Plevna* have all played an important part in the military history of the Balkan Peninsula. *Cettinje*, the former capital of Montenegro, is a mere village. *Durazzo* is the capital of the recently formed state of Albania.

Switzerland.

Position and Extent.

Switzerland is situated in the middle of Europe between France, Germany, Austria, and Italy. It is entirely inland, with an area of 15,976 square miles. The greatest length from east to west is 216 miles, and the width 137 miles.

Surface and General Features.

From a geological point of view there are four
parallel zones extending across the country from south-
west to north-east.   In the north-west is a limestone

A mountain pass in Switzerland.

region consisting of the Jura Mountains, about 3000
feet high.   This is succeeded by the Swiss Plateau,
composed of sandstone and ranging from 1000 to 3000
feet in height.   The rest of Switzerland is occupied by
two Alpine regions, one in the north being of limestone,

and the other, in the middle, formed of crystalline rocks. The Alpine system may be considered under several groups of mountains. The Alpes Vandoises and the Bernese Oberland have more than 20 peaks rising above 12,000 feet, including the Jungfrau and the Wetterhorn, and the longest of all the Swiss glaciers, the Aletsch glacier, 16 miles in length. The other Alpine groups are the Alps of Unterwald with Pilatus (7000 feet), the Alps of Glarus and Schwyz with the Rigi (5906 feet), and the Pennine Alps with Monte Rosa (15,217 feet), the Matterhorn (14,705 feet), and 30 other peaks above 12,000 feet. The other groups may be simply mentioned by name—the Alps of Ticino, the Alps of Grisons, the Bern Alps, and the Jura. The snow-line varies from 9250 feet to 9020 feet, and of upwards of 500 glaciers the canton of Valais claims the largest number.

Rivers and Lakes.

Switzerland is watered by numerous streams which form the head-waters of important rivers—the Rhine, Rhone, Ticino, and Inn. Some of the tributaries of the Rhine come from the St Bernardin and Splügen Passes, and Lake Constance forms part of its course ; but the Aar, its chief Swiss feeder, comes from the Grimsel Pass, flows through the lakes of Brienz and Thun, and drains north Switzerland to the Rhine. The Rhone cuts its way through the Alps to the Furca Pass, and leaves Switzerland after flowing through the Lake of Geneva, the largest of the Swiss lakes. The Ticino flows through Lake Maggiore to the Adriatic, and the Inn to the Danube.

Climate and Natural Productions.

In this country, where the height above sea-level is from 640 feet to the limit of perpetual snow, there is necessarily great variation in the climate. The mean temperature at Bellinzona is 54° F. and at Theodule Pass 20°. The normal temperature diminishes by 3°

for each 1000 feet of elevation. Great extremes of temperature are caused by strong insolation in the day, and considerable variation at night owing to the pure and rare air of the heights. There is much cloudiness, and in the valleys considerable fog. Rain comes with the westerly and southerly winds and some of the windward slopes get 60 inches of rain or even more. Geneva has less than 33 inches. Though not generally favourable to agriculture, the Swiss climate is particularly invigorating and hence draws many visitors who are in search of health.

No less than one-third of the country is classed as unproductive, and only a small portion of the remainder is capable of cultivation. More than one-half of the arable land is devoted to cereals. Tobacco is grown and the vine is cultivated. Dairy products, such as cheese and condensed milk, are of great importance.

People, History, and Industries.

The lake-dwellers of Switzerland were its first inhabitants, but the Helvetians, a Celtic race, were its earliest dwellers in historic times. These people were conquered by the Romans under Julius Caesar, and subsequently the country became part of the German Empire in the eleventh century. The Swiss successfully resisted an attempt by Austria to assert its power over the country ; and the present confederacy of 22 cantons dates from 1350, when a confederation of eight cantons was formed. The neutrality of Switzerland is guaranteed by the European powers. The population of $3\frac{3}{4}$ millions gives a density of about 235 to the square mile. The language varies in different parts. German is the prevailing language, but French and Italian are spoken in the parts adjacent to France and Italy.

Cattle-rearing employs many of the Swiss, and silk and cotton textiles, clocks, and watches are the chief manufactures. The industrial region is in the north, and lies on the great routes by the St Gothard tunnel and Geneva. The centres of the textile industries are

Zurich, Basel, and Glarus. Watch-making is established at Geneva, Neuchatel, and Bern. Wood-carving, first introduced in the Oberland, employs many thousands.

Communications and Trade.

The character of the country presents many obstacles to communication between the different parts of it, and also with the adjacent countries on the south and east. Although there were no carriage roads across the Alps till the beginning of the nineteenth century, there are now some of the finest mountain roads in the world across the Swiss mountains. The Simplon road was opened in 1805, and the St Gothard in 1830. This latter has been largely superseded by one of the longest railway tunnels in the world. Other tunnels have been made, and in 1906 the Simplon tunnel was opened, reducing the distance between Paris and Milan to 519 miles. There are no canals or navigable rivers. Among the exports are silk and cotton goods, embroidery, trimmings, watches, machinery, locomotives, cheese, and condensed milk; the imports are chiefly articles of food and luxury, and raw materials for manufacture.

Administration and Towns.

The Republic of Switzerland became a federal state in 1848. The president is chosen annually, and each canton is a state with a miniature constitution and government. Every citizen has a vote, and the Referendum and the Right of Initiative are two important privileges of the Swiss constitution.

Bern, on the Aar, is the capital. *Zurich*, a railway centre, is the largest town, with most of the textile and transit trade. *Basel*, on the Rhine, has silk weaving. *Geneva*, on the French frontier, has watch and clock-making. *Lausanne* and *Neuchatel* are important trade towns in the west.

Italy.

Position and Extent.

Italy is the second of the three peninsulas of southern Europe and is separated from central Europe on the north by the great mountain barrier of the Alps. The country has well-defined boundaries, for on the other sides it is washed by the sea. Including Sicily, Sardinia, and some smaller islands, the area of Italy is 110,646 square miles, or rather less than that of the British Isles. The greatest length is 710 miles and the breadth varies from 350 miles in the north to 20 miles in the south. To the area of the kingdom of Italy must now be added its colonial possessions in Africa, viz. Eritrea, Italian Somaliland, and Libya, which consists of Tripolitania and Cyrenaica ; and as a result of the Great War Italy has obtained large tracts of former Austrian territory.

Surface and General Features.

Forming the northern boundary, the Alps sweep round in a great curve from Nice to Trieste ; but the highest mountain entirely in Italy is Gran Paradiso (13,652 feet) in Piedmont. South of the Alps is a great alluvial tract, known as the plain of Lombardy. This region, which belongs to the basin of the Po, is fruitful and flourishing, irrigated as it is by numerous streams and canals. Some of the tributaries of the Po expand into lakes of considerable beauty, of which Lago di Garda, Lago Maggiore, and Como are the most noteworthy. From Nice to Spezia the coast region is known as the Riviera, and the mountains come close to the sea. On the other side, from Rimini to Trieste, the coast is flat, marshy, and fringed with lagoons. The long peninsular portion of Italy is traversed by the Apennines, composed of limestone rocks. The highest peak is Monte Corno (9580 feet), and the mean elevation

of the range is not more than 5000 feet. Between the
main chain and the sea on the west coast there is a
volcanic region extending from Tuscany to Vesuvius
(4206 feet), the only active volcano. Etna (10,700 feet)
and Stromboli in the Lipari Islands are other volcanic
centres. The Apennines form the watershed of the
peninsular portion of Italy and the chief rivers flow
into the Tyrrhenian Sea, but only the Tiber and Arno
are navigable for part of their course.

Climate and Rainfall.

The climate of all Mediterranean countries is warm
and dry, but subject to occasional bitterly cold winds
from the Alps and hot dry winds from the African
deserts. Throughout the peninsula the temperature
is lowered by the Apennines, and the Adriatic coast,
exposed to the north-east winds, is colder than corre-
sponding latitudes on the west coast. The plain of
Lombardy, open to the cold winds from the Alps and
closed to those from the south, has a cold short winter.
In some of the marshy districts malaria occurs in the
bad weather from July to October. The highest recorded temperature is 109° F. in Apulia. The Italian
summer is deficient in rain, and winter is the wet season.
The rainfall is heavier on the western than on the eastern
side, and, while the northern region has about 40 inches
yearly, the southern portion has not more than 27
inches.

Productions.

Of the total area of Italy only 10 per cent. is unculti-
vated, and this unproductive portion includes lagoons
and marshes which could be drained and brought
under cultivation. The cultivated area may be considered under five zones. The first comprises the region
which grows oranges, lemons, and similar fruits; it
extends along the southern and western coasts of
Sardinia, comprises a great part of Sicily, and pre-
dominates on the southern Italian coasts past the

gulfs of Salerno and Sorrento to Naples. The wine region of Italy extends over the plains of Lombardy and Emilia, and covers the mountain slopes of Sardinia and Sicily and the whole length of the Apennines. The region of chestnuts extends from the valleys to the plateaux of the Alps, and along the northern slopes of the Apennines, as well as the southern slopes and the ranges of Sicily and Sardinia. The wooded region covers the Alps and the Apennines above the chestnut level. Between the regions of tree culture, cereals, vegetables, and textile plants are cultivated. Cereal cultivation is foremost and wheat is the most important crop. Next come maize, rice, rye, barley, oats, and millet. Pasture occupies about 30 per cent of the cultivated area, and potatoes, turnips, and beetroot are extensively grown. Market-gardening is largely carried on, and the working classes grow white beans and lupins for food and fodder. The chief industrial plant is tobacco, which is a Government monopoly, and the textile plants are hemp, flax, and cotton.

The vine is cultivated throughout the length and breadth of Italy, and the oils obtained from the olive are considered the best in the world. The mulberry tree, whose leaves serve as food for silkworms, is cultivated in every region. Almonds are widely cultivated in Sicily, Sardinia, and the southern provinces, and hazel-nuts, figs, peaches, pears, apples, locust-beans, and pistachio are among other fruits. Good timber is furnished by the oak and beech, and by the pine and fir forests of the mountains.

Numerous varieties of breeds of cattle are distributed throughout Italy, and enormous flocks of sheep are kept by professional sheep-farmers, who pasture them on the mountains in summer and bring them down to the plains in winter. The number of goats is decreasing, but there is an increase in horse-breeding. The north of Italy is famous for its dairy centres, and such cheeses as Parmesan and Gorgonzola are world-famous.

The minerals of Italy are of considerable value. Sulphur is obtained from the volcanic districts, and petroleum is found in central Italy. Iron is mined in Elba, quicksilver and tin in Tuscany, and lead and zinc in Sardinia. Stone quarries are extensively worked, and Italian marble, especially that of Carrara, is exported in large quantities. Lava is used for paving and for building in Sicily and southern Italy.

Industries.

Great progress has been made of late years in the manufacture of machinery, and the importation of coal is very large. Locomotives, railway engines, and electric tramcars are extensively made in the north of Italy and in the vicinity of Naples. Steel rails, armour plates, and ordnance are made at Terni, ships at Leghorn, Genoa, and Naples, motor-cars at Turin, and submarines near Spezia. The silk industry, especially in Lombardy, Piedmont, and Venetia, is thriving, and there is scarcely a family of peasants that does not breed silkworms. The cotton industry is developing, and among other textile industries are those connected with wool, flax, and jute. Chemical industries show an output of over £2,000,000 per year, and match-making is a flourishing Italian industry with 200 factories. Straw-plaiting is a characteristic Florentine industry, and paper-making and furniture-making are noteworthy. Italy has a foremost place in artistic industries, and fine glass, beautiful china-ware, jewellery, and lace-making are carried on with great success. Italian fisheries have greatly developed. Most of the fishing boats start from the Adriatic coast, the coral boats from the western coast, and the sponge boats from Sicily and the west coast. Tunny, anchovies, and sardines are largely caught and exported.

People and History.

There is a great contrast between the people in north and south Italy, and this may be accounted for by the fact that Phoenicians, Greeks, Berbers, and Arabs from the south were brought into contact with Slavs, Germans, and Celts from the north in the Roman period, when all the groups adopted the Latin language. Down to the present day the Italians have a remarkable unity of speech, but, of the various dialects, Tuscan is the purest form of the language. The population of Italy is 36,000,000, and there is yearly a large emigration to foreign lands, especially to North and South America. Italy was first united by Rome, on whose fall Charlemagne became its ruler. Spain, France, and Austria have also had rule over portions of Italy, but in all periods of her history Italian influence on the world has been marked. Especially was this the case in the Middle Ages, when intellectually, and commercially, Italy took the lead among European nations. It was not till 1862, however, that modern Italy was constituted, and in 1870 the Papal States were added, and Rome became the capital. During the succeeding 50 years the political conditions of Italy have been improved, and great progress has been made in every direction. Specially noteworthy is the evident desire of the Italian people for expansion, and this has resulted in the conquest of Tripoli.

The Roman Catholic religion is recognised by the state and claims almost the whole of the people. The Pope is a sovereign prince, although his temporal possessions have been lost to the state. Nearly all the religious houses have been suppressed.

Trade and Communications.

Italian trade with foreign countries amounted in 1920 to upwards of £634,000,000, with an excess of imports over exports of £320,000,000. The commercial development of Italy is apparent when we note that this foreign trade has more than trebled in 6 years. During the last 40 years Italy has been transformed from a purely agricultural country into a largely in-

dustrial country, so that trade in raw stuffs and manufactured articles exceeds that in food products. Silk is
the most important export, and cotton is the chief item
in Italian imports. Cattle are largely imported, and
dairy and farm products, especially eggs and cheese,
are valuable exports. Wheat and maize are imported
from Russia and Rumania, and macaroni is sent to
the United States and Great Britain. Wine, oranges,
lemons, and fresh vegetables are exported in large
quantities, and, while rubber is purchased from Brazil
and the Congo, Italy sends away increasing values of
rubber tyres and motor-cars. The trade with Great
Britain and the United States is very large and shows
a tendency to expand.

The railway system leading to Italy is unique
on account of the many long tunnels. The most
important lines are by the Mont Cenis from France,
tho Simplon from Switzerland and France, the St
Gothard from Switzerland and Germany, and the
Brenner Pass, which crosses the Alps without a tunnel,
from Austria and Eastern Germany. There are now
upwards of 10,000 miles of railway, the greater part
being owned by the state. The Sicilian railways
are connected with the system of the mainland by
ferry-boats, on which through-carriages from Reggio
to Messina are conveyed across the Straits.

Administration.

The government is a limited monarchy, and there
are two houses of parliament. Italy is divided into
69 provinces and 214 territories.

Towns.

The capital is *Rome*, the "Eternal City," formerly
the centre of the ancient Roman republic and of the
Roman empire, and the headquarters of the Christian
Church. It is unique among the historical cities of
the world and its remains comprise ancient walls and

Rome: the walls of Aurelian.

buildings, the fora, baths, and arches. The galleries and
collections of Rome are the largest in the world, and the
Vatican, the Lateran, the Capitoline, and the National
Museums have priceless treasures of art. Rome is
rapidly growing in population and its industries are
increasing. *Milan*, the junction for the St Gothard
railway, is the great centre of the silk trade. *Turin*,
the capital of Piedmont, is the centre of the motor-car
industry. *Florence*, on both banks of the Arno, is the
chief town of Tuscany and the richest city in the world
in collections of works of artistic interest. At *Venice*
are the famous St Mark's and the Doge's Palace. The city
is built on 120 islets and was once the chief commercial
city of the world. *Genoa* is the chief port of Italy. Its
growth is due to the opening of the Alpine tunnels, so
that it now competes with Marseilles. *Leghorn*, the
chief seaport of Tuscany, has a flourishing trade and is
an important ship-building centre. *Palermo*, the capital
of Sicily, is a favourite winter resort and the chief
seaport of the island, exporting oranges, lemons, and
other fruits. *Cagliari*, the capital of Sardinia, is built
on a precipitous hill and overlooks a bay.

The Maltese Islands.

This group consists of Malta and Gozo, and some
smaller islands. Malta is about 60 miles from Sicily
and 200 miles from Cape Bon in Africa. It is the
headquarters of the British Mediterranean fleet and
the principal coasting station in the Mediterranean :
and owing to the enormous strength of its fortifications,
it is a very important British dependency, securing
as it does the route to India by the Suez Canal. Malta
came into our possession during the Napoleonic wars
and was transferred to Britain by the Treaty of Paris
in 1814. The island is densely inhabited by nearly
230,000 people, many of whom speak a debased Arabic,
although the upper classes speak Italian. Large

crops of wheat and potatoes are grown, and fruits and flowers are plentiful. Filigree ornaments are made by the people and cotton is manufactured to a small extent. *Valetta*, the capital, is a powerful stronghold, and the Governor's palace was formerly that of the Order of St John, to whom the island belonged for nearly 300 years.

The Iberian Peninsula.

Position and Extent.

The Iberian Peninsula, which comprises Spain and Portugal, has an area of 230,172 square miles, of which Portugal has about one-sixth. This southwestern peninsula of southern Europe is cut off from the mainland by the Pyrenees, and its shores are washed by the Bay of Biscay, the Atlantic, and the Mediterranean. This peninsula has been well described as " a world in itself " and " a world of contradictions," and it has been remarked that although the sea surrounds seven-eighths of its periphery, it has all the features of a continental mass with restricted access to the ocean.

Surface and General Features.

Reference to the map will show that this pentagonal mass terminates on its seaward faces in a high and regular coast-line. There are few inlets on the coast ; the rivers are only partly navigable ; and there are not many off-lying islands. The Pyrenees, separating Spain from France, are continued westwards by the Cantabrian and Esturian Mountains, which form the northern boundary of a tableland covering the greater part of the peninsula with an average height of 2700 feet. The tableland is bordered everywhere, except in the west, by mountains and steep slopes. The highest peaks are Maladetta (11,170 feet) in the

Pyrenees and Mulhaçen (11,530 feet) in the Sierra Nevada.

The rivers of the peninsula are of considerable length, but are so obstructed by rapids and shallows as to be of little use in navigation, and their beds lie in deep valleys far below the level of the tableland. The Guadalquivir is the most important of the rivers as regards navigability, and the level of its water is fairly uniform. The Ebro has the largest basin and is the only navigable river on the east side.

Climate and Rainfall.

The regular character of the coast-line and the great elevation of the plateau give Spain a more continental character in its extreme range of temperature than any other European peninsula. The western side of the plateau is more humid and much colder than the eastern. In the interior the air is everywhere dry, and the coast-strip between Gibraltar and Almeria has the warmest winter climate of Europe. The climate of Madrid is the most extreme in Western Europe; the mean temperature ranges from 36° in January to 76° in July. In summer the temperature may rise to 107° F. in the shade, and in winter skating is not uncommon. Rainfall is most abundant in the coastal regions, and as a rule it diminishes from north-west to south-east. The total annual rainfall is less than 20 inches over most of the peninsula, and the height of summer is a period of extreme drought, more especially in the southern part.

Productions and Industries.

Although mining and other industries are developing, agriculture is the mainstay of the people; it is estimated that nearly 70 per cent. of the people are engaged in it. A good deal of the country is arid, and at least 4000 square miles are artificially irrigated at great expense. The "huertas" (gardens) of Valencia and Murcia are nourished in this way and yield southern fruits of all kinds and mulberries, as well as rice and maize. Oranges are grown at no great distance from the coast; the sugar-cane is cultivated in Granada, Malaga, and Almeria ; and the vine thrives. The chief Portuguese wines (port etc.) come from the valley of the Douro, and the Spanish wine (sherry) is made in the south. Spanish wool, once so famous throughout Europe, no longer ranks so high in quality. Wheat, barley, rye, and maize are the chief grain crops for home consumption, and chick-peas, onions, and garlic are largely grown for exportation. The cork-oak yields the most important forest product, and the olive abounds in the southern part of the peninsula.

The mineral wealth of Spain is considerable but not fully developed. Iron-ore of excellent quality is mined near Bilbao, Corunna, and Almeria. Lead and silver are associated at Linares, and Almaden has one of the chief quicksilver mines in the world. The principal copper mines are at Rio Tinto, and bay-salt is produced on the southern coasts of both Spain and Portugal.

The manufactures include cotton and other textile goods in Catalonia; and there are iron industries in the neighbourhood of the iron mines. There is some leather work, esparto-plaiting, silk-spinning, and weaving, and at some of the seaports ship-building is carried on.

People and History.

The people are of mixed race, but the Iberians were probably the earliest inhabitants of the peninsula, and the Basques in the north-east are their descendants. The Celts gained a footing in the north-west, and the Romans civilised the whole country. The Goths invaded the land, and the invasion of the Arabs and Moors in the eighth century had great effect on the country, as regards the physical type of the people, their customs, and the geographical names. It was not till 1492 that the Moors were finally conquered; and Spain became one Christian Kingdom in 1512. Spain and Portugal were great European nations in the fifteenth and sixteenth centuries. For about 100 years Spain was mistress of the world; but the pride of the ruling classes has probably been the cause of the decadence of both countries. The history of Spain in the nineteenth century sank to its lowest with the loss of its American and eastern colonies. Spain, with a population of 20 millions, is a limited monarchy with two houses of parliament (Cortes). Portugal, with 6 million people, became a republic in 1910.

Trade and Communications.

The trade of both countries is similar. Iron-ore and wine are the chief Spanish exports, and lead, copper, and quicksilver, as well as southern fruits, cork, and paper are also of some importance. Spain imports raw cotton, wheat, coal, and timber. France, England, and the United States are Spain's best customers. Figs, cork, and copper-ore are among the chief exports of Portugal. The United Kingdom and Brazil have the largest share of Portuguese trade. The roads of Spain and Portugal are not good, and the country, from its mountainous character, is unfavourable to internal communications. The Pyrenees are as yet uncrossed by any railway, and there are so many obstacles that little progress is likely to be made with railway construction.

Towns of Spain.

Madrid, the capital, in New Castile, is the chief railway centre. *Barcelona* has been for centuries the chief seaport and industrial town. *Valencia, Cartagena, Malaga,* and *Seville* are all important seaports and industrial towns. *Cadiz* has a fine harbour, but the trade is declining. *Huelva* exports copper to Britain. *Bilbao* ships iron-ore and has a large foreign trade.

Towns of Portugal.

Lisbon, on the Tagus, is the capital and chief seaport. *Oporto,* on the Douro, is the second port, with a large wine trade. *Setubal,* the third port, has salt-works.

Cadiz.

Gibraltar.

Gibraltar, at the southern extremity of Spain, is a celebrated fortress which has belonged to Britain since 1704. Its importance lies in the fact that it dominates the entrance to the Mediterranean, and the fortifications, constructed at enormous cost, may be considered impregnable. It is an important coaling station as well as a naval station, and recently much has been done to improve the harbour accommodation. The area of this fortress, situated on a rocky promontory, 1408 feet high, is 1266 acres. The population, including the military, is about 27,000. Gibraltar is within four days of England and is a free port.

QUESTIONS

AND

EXERCISES

General Features

1. Give some figures to show the extent of Europe. What is the origin of the word "Europe"?

2. Locate the three groups of European volcanoes, and name the districts where there are extinct volcanoes.

3. Where are the following lakes: Como, Balaton, Neagh, Wener? Briefly describe one of them.

4 Which of the European seas are tideless? Why?

5. Name the chief islands in the Mediterranean Sea.

6. What do you know about the distribution of the rainfall in Europe?

7. Read the section on the "Economic Resources of Europe," pp. 128–9, and then write a summary of it.

8. Where is the population of Europe (a) sparse, (b) dense? Account for the facts in each case.

9. What are the chief races of people in Europe and where is each found?

10. Mention in order the chief natural features in a coasting voyage from Bordeaux to Hamburg; also mention political divisions, towns, and anything of special interest.

11. Give the exact position and account for the importance of Brindisi, the Kiel Canal, Malta, Metz, Pola.

12. Give some account of the Black Earth Region, the Karst, the Landes, the Mer de Glace, the Riviera, the Tirol.

13. Contrast the climates of Glasgow and Moscow as regards (*a*) summer temperature, (*b*) winter temperature, (*c*) rainfall, accounting for the differences that are found.

14. What is the latitude of Moscow, and what is the time there when it is noon at Greenwich?

15. Draw a sketch-map of the North Sea coast-line from Pentland Firth to Dover, and from Calais to the Skaw. Name and mark the positions of Buchan Ness, the Dogger Bank, the Frisian Islands, the Goodwin Sands, Calais, Harwich, Heligoland.

FRANCE

1. What are the facts relating to the extent of France in (*a*) Europe, (*b*) Asia, (*c*) Africa?

2. Where are Brittany, the Riviera, the Auvergne, the Cotentin peninsula?

3. Compare the climate of France with that of England.

4. Where are the vine, olive, and mulberry trees grown in France? Name the wine-producing districts.

5. Make a list of the chief industries of France and state where each is carried on.

6. On an outline map of France mark the chief railway lines.

7. What do you know of the history of France during the last 50 years?

8. Where are the following towns and for what are they famous: Reims, Dunkirk, Cherbourg, Strassburg, Dieppe?

9. Draw a map of Corsica and show its position with regard to (*a*) France, (*b*) Italy.

10. Compare the density to the square mile of the French population with that of the British.

BELGIUM

1. Describe the surface and general features of Belgium.

2. What are the chief minerals of Belgium, and where are they found?

3. Why have many Belgian towns a Flemish as well as a French name?

4. When and why were Belgium and Holland separated?

5. Account for the importance of Antwerp and Ostend, and mention with what English ports they trade.

6. Name six large towns in Belgium and describe three of them.

HOLLAND

1. What is the official name of Holland? What is its extent?

2. What do you know of the dykes and canals of Holland?

3. Where are the Zuider Zee and the Dollart Zee? How were they formed?

4. What are the chief occupations of the Dutch?

5. With what countries does Holland trade? What articles are exported?

6. Write a few notes about Amsterdam, Flushing, The Hague, Delft.

GERMANY

1. What was the extent of Germany (a) before, (b) after the Great War?

2. Name the most important mountains of Germany, and the two highest peaks.

3. Where is the "Kaiser Wilhelm Canal"? Why was it constructed, and what is the provision of the Treaty of Versailles with regard to its future use?

4. Contrast the lakes of Germany in the south and in the north.

5. What are the wild animals found in Germany?

6. Where are potatoes, wheat, sugar-beet, flax, the vine, grown in Germany?

7. Compare the population of Germany with that of France, as regards the density to the square mile and the rate of increase.

8. What industries are associated with Hamburg, Bavaria, Saxony, Nuremburg, Munich?

9. When was the German Empire formed? When did Germany become a Republic?

10. For what are the following towns famous: Leipzig, Cologne, Kiel, Danzig, Chemnitz?

Denmark

1. What do you know of the recent history of Sleswig and Holstein?

2. Draw a map of Denmark, name the islands, and show the position of Sweden and Norway.

3. "Denmark is essentially an agricultural country." Explain and illustrate this statement.

4. When did Denmark cease to rule Sweden, Norway, and Iceland?

Scandinavia

1. What is meant by Scandinavia? Give some facts relating to its extent.

2. Describe the coasts of (a) Norway, (b) Sweden.

3. Name the chief rivers of Scandinavia and discuss their value for purposes of navigation.

4. Compare the climate of Norway and Sweden.

5. What are the chief resources of Norway? Why is shipbuilding an important industry?

6. When and why did Norway separate from Sweden?

7. Write a few notes on the Maelström, Upsala, Goteborg, Hammerfest, Malmo.

8. Show how the differences of country influence the lives and occupations of the Norwegians and Swedes.

Russia

1. What changes have taken place in the government of Russia since the Great War? Name any states that have been formed from this country.

2. What are the characteristics of the Russian rivers? Draw a map of the Volga and mark six towns on its banks.

3. "The climate of Russia is continental." Explain this statement.

4. Why is agriculture the chief occupation of the Russians? Where are the industrial centres?

5 Where are the following towns and for what are they famous: Odessa, Sebastopol, Archangel, Astrakhan, Baku, Riga?

FINLAND

1. Describe briefly the surface and extent of Finland.
2. What are the manufactures and exports of Finland?
3. When was Finland joined to Russia? When did it become a republic?
4. Name three of the chief towns in Finland and write a few notes on each.

AUSTRIA AND HUNGARY

1. Compare the extent of these states before and after the Great War.
2. Write a few notes on the Fata Morgana, the Föhn, Lake Balaton.
3. Give some account of the mineral resources of Austria and Hungary.
4. Name the chief Austrian tunnels through the Alps and show their advantages for purposes of travel.
5. Name the capitals of these two states and describe their position and characteristics.
6. Why are there so few large towns on the Danube below Budapest?

POLAND

1. What is the extent of Poland, and what are the neighbouring states?
2. Write a few notes on the history of Poland? When was its independence acknowledged?
3. Mention three of the largest towns of Poland, and write a few sentences about the capital.

CZECHO-SLOVAKIA

1. What are the states that are comprised in this country?
2. Give some account of the population of this country, specially with reference to race and religion.
3. Describe the position and importance of Prague, Bono, Olmütz.

RUMANIA

1. Draw an outline map of Rumania, and on it mark the chief divisions.

2. Describe the course of the Danube through Rumania, and give some notes on the Dobruja.

3. Trace the development of Rumania since 1878.

4. Write a few sentences about Bukharest, Jassy, Galatz.

The Balkan Peninsula

1. What are the states within this region? What is their extent?

2. Write a short account of the climate and show how it affects the products of this area.

3. Give some account of the character of the communications in the Balkan Peninsula.

4. Read the section on p. 189 on the Geographical Character of Greece, and then write the substance of it from memory.

5. Describe the position and importance of Athens, Corinth, Patras, Constantinople, Salonika.

Switzerland

1. What are some of the groups in the Alpine system? Name the chief peaks with their heights.

2. Describe the rivers and lakes of Switzerland.

3. Mention some of the Swiss industries and say where they are carried on.

4. Write a few notes on the communications and trade of Switzerland.

Italy

1. What is the extent of Italy? Name its possessions in Africa.

2. On an outline map of Italy mark the Alps, the Apennines, and four peaks.

3. Give a full account of the productions of Italy.

4. What do you know of the history of Italy since 1862?

5. By what tunnels do the various railway lines enter Italy from (a) France, (b) Switzerland, (c) Austria?

6. Describe the following towns and show their importance: Rome, Florence, Milan, Turin, Genoa, Palermo.

THE IBERIAN PENINSULA

1. Give a short account of the position and extent of this region.

2. Draw a map of Spain and Portugal and mark on it the chief mountains and rivers.

3. Why is the climate of Madrid subject to extremes?

4. What are the chief agricultural and mineral productions of Spain and Portugal?

5. At what period of their history were Spain and Portugal flourishing? How do you account for their decadence?

6. Write a few lines about Gibraltar and discuss its importance.

7. Give the position of the following towns and describe their importance: Barcelona, Cadiz, Oporto, Santander, Seville.

For EU product safety concerns, contact us at Calle de José Abascal, 56–1°,
28003 Madrid, Spain or eugpsr@cambridge.org.

www.ingramcontent.com/pod-product-compliance
Ingram Content Group UK Ltd.
Pitfield, Milton Keynes, MK11 3LW, UK
UKHW012333130625
459647UK00009B/267